First-Time Japan

A STEP-BY-STEP GUIDE FOR THE INDEPENDENT TRAVELER

Enoshima Island with the Enoshima Sea Candle lighthouse peeking out above the summit.

First-Time Japan

A STEP-BY-STEP GUIDE FOR THE INDEPENDENT TRAVELER

BY **SNEED B. COLLARD III**

with Roy Ozaki

Missoula, Montana

Cover photo: Kiyomizu-dera Temple, Kyoto.

Cover and book design by Jeannie Painter.
The text of this book is set in Berthold Akzidenz Grotesk 22.

DISTRIBUTED BY:
Mountain Press Publishing Company
Missoula, Montana
800-234-5308 • www.mountain-press.com

Name: Collard, Sneed B., author.
Title: First-Time Japan: A Step-by-Step Guide for the Independent Traveler / Sneed B. Collard III. / with Roy Ozaki.
Description: Missoula, Montana : Bucking Horse Books
Summary: With its incredible cuisine, majestic scenery, and vibrant culture, Japan promises the trip of a lifetime to the independent traveler. That said, many would-be visitors find the prospect of a Japanese adventure, well, intimidating. The significant language barrier, complicated subway system, and sheer immensity of Tokyo and other large Japanese cities can strike trepidation into the heart of even an experienced traveler. *First-Time Japan* cuts through both the fear and the overwhelming complication of traditional travel guides, and lays out an enjoyable, step-by-step strategy for planning your first trip.
Identifiers: LCCN 2023947366 / ISBN 978-1-7328753-2-6 (paperback)
Subjects: Japan–Guidebooks. / Japan–Description and Travel.
Classification: 915.2045

Manufactured in the United States of America

10 9 8 7 6 5 4 3 2 1

For Tessa

Love,
Daddo

Hachiko Memorial, Shibuya Station.

CONTENTS

An iconic Tokyo landmark, Tokyo Tower is a popular—though optional—tourist attraction.

INTRODUCTION

This is (mostly) Not a Sightseeing Guide

If you are contemplating a trip to Japan, chances are you already have a good idea what you'd like to see and experience. If you don't—but still want to go anyway—many excellent Japan travel books, websites, blogs, and social media pages await you, and can advise you on everything from famous sights to see to where and what to eat.

This book is not one of those—at least not for the most part.

This guide's primary goal is to provide concise information on how to plan and negotiate your first trip to Japan as an independent traveler, no matter how you want to do it or what you want to see. Because let's face it: Japan is no ordinary travel destination. Its people are different. Its transportation is different. Most of all, the language is all but impenetrable for the vast majority of earth's inhabitants. All of these are *great* reasons to go—but can be a source of anxiety, or at least nervous excitement, for first-time visitors. And while standard Japan guidebooks will tell you what to do, including sections on transportation and so forth, in preparing for my first trip I found that almost all of them either

a) had gaping holes in providing critical, specific details

and/or

b) provided so *many* details that they contradicted themselves or created enough confusion as to be practically worthless.

This book seeks to cut through those problems. The following chapters *will* include sights, foods, and other experiences that my teen and I particularly enjoyed—and yes, Japan is a *great* place to take your teen—but my overriding goal is to provide the step-by-step details and clear information you need to plan a unique adventure for you and any companions you choose to bring along. You'll find that I devote the greatest number of words to transportation, probably the most intimidating aspect of Japan for most travelers. However, I'll also plunge into choosing when to go, booking accommodations, finding food, negotiating the language, and perhaps most important, creating your own personalized itinerary.

The actual planning will be up to you, but hey, that is part of the fun! The process of selecting where you want to go and what you want to see will teach you a lot about the country and pump up your excitement to visit even more. How great is that?

To help provide an authentic Japanese perspective for all of the above topics, I've been fortunate to enlist the help of **Ryosuke ("Roy") Ozaki**. Roy has worked as a tour guide in Japan for years, and has helped show hundreds of visitors the best Japan has to offer. Throughout this book, he shares his insights, tips, and knowledge to help you make the most of your trip.

So without further ado, let's dive in, beginning with just why you should visit the Land of the Rising Sun.

Enoshima-jinja Shrine, Enoshima Island.

View of Tokyo Bay from Tokyo Tower.

PART I

Embracing the Big Picture

楽

Why Go?

As mentioned before, you probably have a pretty solid idea of why you want to visit Japan. You may be a fan of Japanese cuisine and want to eat so much of it that you can enter a sumo wrestling tournament. Perhaps you just love temples and castles and museums, all of which Japan has in abundance, or have heard about its beautiful national parks and hot springs. Maybe you want to shop till you drop or are wondering what it's like to live in a country where decisions are often made for the common good above the individual. Or perhaps you would like to visit a festival or experience a different, perhaps more positive, spiritual ethos than is found in your own native land.

When my teen, Tessa, and I first began dreaming about Japan, many factors drove our imaginations. We had both became enamored with Japan's cuisine but Tessa also wanted to spend more time in big cities, something in short supply in our home state of Montana. I, too, was interested in Japan's cities–but more in how the Japanese designed them to be efficient, especially in regard to their legendary transportation system. Pop culture drew both of us, whether it was

People visit Japan for many reasons, including just soaking up the everyday rhythm of the country at public places such as Kyoto's Kamo River.

the movies of Studio Ghibli, the art of anime and manga, or Netflix shows such as *Terrace House* and *Tokyo Diner*, which we watched with fascination.

But while we did want to visit a few temples, we didn't want to experience Japan as sightseers *per se*. Except for the manga museum in Kyoto, for instance, Tessa made it clear that museums held absolutely no interest for her, and I happily went along with that philosophy, having spent far too much time in museums on other trips. Food, though, assumed a top priority as did spending time outdoors, especially places that might have birds. In fact, I was getting dangerously close to reaching 1,000 species on my birding life list, and I hoped that Japan might just put me over the top![1]

Beyond all of this, the mystery of the country attracted us—and, I've found, draws other people as well. What was this country really like, a country that had lived through centuries of isolation, then rose to become a military power with ambitions to rule half the world—only to suffer absolute defeat before becoming one of the world's great economic powers? What were its people like *today* and how did they go about their normal routines? How did religion infuse their lives and shape the country they are creating?

We didn't expect more than hints at the answers to these questions, but they were glimpses we wanted to experience. I'm guessing they are a part of why you want to visit Japan, too. No matter your thoughts and reasoning, or what made you finally buy this book, I can confidently predict that if you make an effort to dive a bit below the surface, your decision to visit Japan will enrich the rest of your life. Still, you may feel a bit overwhelmed at the idea, so let's address that first.

Wrapping Your Mind Around It

I gotta admit that I'm astonished by how many people seem to hesitate at the thought of visiting Japan. Here in my home state of Montana, gobs of folks visit Hawai'i, Mexico, Spain, and other places. Mention Japan, though, and chances are they will look at you like you are proposing a trip to Mars. Even people who want to go to Japan

[1] I got close, reaching 996!

often feel intimidated by the country. Let's call it "Fear of Japan." I do get it. A glance at the Japanese written language or a Tokyo subway map can make the most intrepid traveler take pause, thinking, *Uh, maybe this is beyond my abilities.*

Let me assure you, it is not.

For me, there are two keys to traveling Japan. One is simply accepting the fact that it's going to be different—just like any other foreign country. For instance, you'll have to learn how to use those famous Japanese toilets. You'll have to learn the transportation system. Unless you've been studying it, you will *not* be able to learn much of the language, so you'll have to work around that. All of this is well within your capabilities.

The second key is that the more you prepare, the better your trip will be. I have traveled more than thirty countries on six continents, but have never been to a country that rewards travel planning better than Japan does. Sure, you can just parachute into Tokyo or Kyoto and have a wonderful experience—but you will waste a lot of time, money, and effort figuring out the basics.

If you are still on the fence about visiting, let me point out one, often unreported fact that may sway you. *Japan is actually easier to travel than most other countries.* Here are just a few reasons why:

- Crime is almost nonexistent unless you happen to be a member of the yakuza or an international crime syndicate.
- English signage is common—or at least common enough.
- The transportation, as complicated as it seems, is a joy to use once you get the hang of it.
- The food is both tasty and abundant.
- Tap water is safe to drink.
- Japanese people, while not especially outgoing toward strangers, are considerate and kind—and always willing to help.
- And did I already mention those amazing Japanese toilets?

The bottom line (pun intended) is that not only can you handle Japan, you will love doing so. Before proceeding, though, let's talk about whether you can afford it.

Food often sits at the top of the list of reasons to visit Japan.

Calculating a Ballpark Budget

Obviously, by the time you read this, almost anything I say about prices will be out of date. How much you budget for your trip will depend on your traveling style, how many people are going, the timing of your visit (think seasons, pandemics, and holidays), the dollar-to-yen exchange rate, any special events happening in the country, and other factors, many of which are beyond your control. I will say that Japan in general proved less expensive than I expected. Our flights took the biggest chunk of our budget—almost two thousand dollars each when we traveled—but your cost will depend greatly on when you go and from where.

Tessa and I were fortunate to visit Japan immediately following its "re-opening" from covid. Once in the country, we found hotels, food, and transportation quite a bit cheaper than what we'd find in an ordinary American city—and much cheaper than in, say, New York or San Francisco. Unfortunately, it seems that as soon as the Japanese realized that tourists fully intended to come back, prices jumped. Many hotels jacked up their prices and the cost of Japan Rail Passes soared a lofty 70% or so. If you plan to cover a lot of ground, however, the Japan Rail Pass remains a solid deal, and many hotels can still be found at decent prices, even in Tokyo.

I've always found that a good overall strategy for planning any big trip is to tally up what you *think* you're going to spend—and then add 50%. This again proved true for Japan. Four years before we visited the country, I set aside $10,000 for the entire trip—and when we finally got to travel there in 2023, that proved very close to the mark. Our three-week trip for two people ended up costing just short of $11,000, and this included some unexpected expenses. As I'll explain later, for instance, I bought separate airline tickets to get us from Montana to Seattle, and then from Seattle to Tokyo. This necessitated an extra overnight hotel in Seattle. Because we traveled just after Japan re-opened from covid, unexpected cancellations or illness seemed like a possibility so I also went ahead and shelled out $500 for trip insurance.

All that said, I predict you'll find Japan to be reasonably-priced once you get over there—especially if you eat local, take advantage of their wonderful public transportation system, and stay away from large Western hotel chains. You will especially save money if you go during an off season—but you may have to put up with some inclement weather and miss out on certain peak season events. **For more on calculating costs, see "Part II: A Japan Game Plan, Step by Step," and "Japan Book & Website Travel Resources" at the back of this book.**

Though prices can fluctuate wildly with seasons and pandemics, we found that once we got there, costs of hotels, transportation, and food in Japan proved comparable to the U.S. or Europe—and sometimes much cheaper.

Passports, Visas, Vaccinations, Money, and Insurance

To complete Big Picture considerations, it's not a bad idea to review just what documents and financial tools you'll need for your trip—including actually entering the country. Let's take them step by step.

PASSPORTS AND VISAS

One wonderful thing about Japan is that, at least at the time of this writing, few documents are required to visit. The most important, of course, is a valid passport. With that, if you're an American citizen, you can take advantage of the good relations between our countries and dispense with getting a visa ahead of time. As long as you are there only for tourism, Japanese authorities will issue you a valid visa upon your arrival in the country. As always, though, check the latest regulations online well before your visit. An excellent site for this and other information is the **Japan National Tourism Organization** (or "**Japan Travel**") website:

➤ *www.japan.travel/en/*

VACCINATIONS

In addition to your passport it's a good idea to bring your vaccination records. Japan, in general, is a very safe country regarding risk of disease, but many basic vaccinations are recommended by the **Centers for Disease Control and Prevention**, or **CDC**. The current list can be found at:

➤ *wwwnc.cdc.gov/travel/destinations/traveler/none/japan*

More information can be found at the **Japan Travel** website:

➤ *www.japan.travel/en/guide/vaccines-for-japan/*

The above sites make a couple of things evident. First, Japan does not require any specialized vaccines, but does recommend the basic ones as listed. Second, the covid situation will continue to be fluid. Even if Japan does not require it at the time of your visit, in this pandemic-era world, it's only prudent to carry a card proving that you have received the most recent complement of covid vaccinations. (**See also the chapter on vaccinations in "Part VII: Health and Hygiene."**)

ENTERING THE COUNTRY

Japan has streamlined the actual entry process by allowing you to upload essential documents ahead of time using **Japan Web**. Here, you can scan and upload your airline ticket and passport, and they will issue you a QR code that you show upon your arrival. We did not use this before our visit, but the airport provided numerous, helpful assistants who walked us through the process once we arrived. It alleviates stress to do this ahead of time, however. The latest instructions can be found by looking up Japan Web online:
➤ *vjw-lp.digital.go.jp/en/*

MONEY

In addition to your essential documents, you will also want to make sure you have at least two credit cards and a bank card that allows you to withdraw money from your account in the form of Japanese yen. And in case you are wondering, yes, ATMs are abundant in Japan and distributed throughout the country. We never found ourselves more than a block or two from one. Be warned that many Japanese businesses–especially food vendors and smaller restaurants–only take cash, so it's a good idea to carry twenty or thirty thousand yen (a couple of hundred bucks) around with you at all times. It's also a good idea to carry enough U.S. dollars with you to survive for a few days in case of emergencies. **(See "Connections & Cash" in Part IV.)**

HEALTH INSURANCE

Speaking of emergencies, you want to make sure you have health insurance coverage while traveling. Japan has excellent health care, but it's not free. Many U.S. health plans, including my own, have no or insufficient coverage for travelers. For others, you may have to pay any bills up-front and pray that you get reimbursed later. Be sure to check your own policy and call a rep if necessary. If your plan leaves you feeling less than secure, consider springing for traveler's insurance. The extra money is well-spent for the peace of mind it provides.

Kamakura's bronze statue of Amida Buddha, or "Buddha of Infinite Light," is Japan's second tallest bronze buddha statue and well worth a visit. It was cast in 1252 and has survived multiple disasters.

PART II

A Japan Game Plan, Step by Step

楽

A Planning Strategy

Now that you have an overall sense of what you'll need to visit, it's time to eagerly rub your hands together and dig into the actual planning of your adventure. Planning for Japan is in many ways similar to planning for any other trip. Seasonal weather patterns will dramatically impact your experience there. Many important events, such as festivals, also happen only at certain times of the year–and require advance planning to experience. *One big difference in planning for Japan, however, is that studying your intended locations and transportation options will streamline your trip even more than it will for other countries.* Given all this, it's a great idea to come up with an overall strategy. Below is the one that my daughter and I used for creating our own Japan trip, and I highly recommend it as you begin planning for one of your own great adventures.

Step 1: Decide what you most want to see and experience, including which cities or regions you want to visit.

Step 2: Decide how much time you have to spend.

Step 3: Choose a season to visit, then buy your airline tickets.

Step 4: Familiarize yourself with the basic transportation system.

Step 5: Group your daily activities by location and book your lodging.

Step 6: Reserve tickets for specialized events and sights.

Step 7: Create a detailed day-by-day itinerary.

Step 8: Purchase your Japan Rail Pass vouchers–if desired.

You, of course, will want to study up on other details such as food and language, but those fall under the category of "Phase II Research" and we'll delve into them later. Before we discuss the above steps in detail, however, you are probably asking yourself: **"How far in advance should I begin planning?"**

My answer: as early as you can–and my collaborator Roy Ozaki agrees, adding, "Timing is everything."

Because of the covid situation, Tessa and I weren't able to begin our serious planning process until about six months prior to our visit–but I recommend starting a year in advance if at all possible. During peak seasons, for example, hotels fill up extremely early, and could get a lot more expensive if you wait to book them. Your timing, though, will depend on your comfort with uncertainty. If you're a last-minute type of person and have plenty of loose cash, hey, have at it, and the best of luck to you. For most people, a trip to Japan is a significant investment and they will want to make sure they're not left scrambling for reservations or paying inflated, last-minute prices.

With that, let's tackle each step in the planning process to help ensure you build a rock-solid foundation for what may become an adventure of a lifetime.

STEP 1
CHOOSE WHAT YOU WANT TO SEE AND DO

As it would be for any other country, the first step in planning your trip to Japan is deciding what you want to do there. Most people want to see various temples and shrines, eat Japanese food, visit museums, and ride a bullet train, but you also probably have other things in mind. For instance, you may want to go skiing or visit Studio Ghibli. You may have your heart set on soaking in *onsen*[2], or hot springs, or watching a sumo wrestling competition. There also may be certain festivals and other events that you want to attend—events that happen only at specific times of the year.

Personally, I wanted to go birding as much as possible while Tessa wanted to learn more about anime and just experience big city life. This is where traditional guidebooks come in handy. You'll want to pick up a couple of different books, such as Fodor's *Essential Japan*, Lonely Planet's *Japan*, or the more simplified *Things I Wish I Knew Before Going to Japan*, and read through them to give you a better idea of what's available and where things are located. Online blogs, websites, and other resources also abound to assist you. **(For specific recommendations, see "Japan Book & Website Travel Resources" at the end of this book.)**

Our own list of things to do in Japan included:

- Eat lots of different Japanese foods.
- Have some nice interactions with Japanese people.
- Visit the statue of Hachiko.

[2] The term onsen refers both to actual hot springs, and to structures and public bath houses containing them.

- Explore a market or two.
- Go to Tokyo Tower.
- Visit Tokyo Disney.
- Hit some big video game centers.
- Attend a Japanese baseball game.
- Visit some temples and shrines.
- Go to a sumo wrestling match.
- Visit Studio Ghibli.
- Stroll some big outdoor parks.
- Shop.
- See a movie in a theater.
- Rent bicycles.
- Go birding.
- Enjoy the sakura (Japanese cherry) blossoms.

Seeing birds featured highly on my list of things to do in Japan.

Seeing a baseball game in Tokyo Dome proved one of our most fun Japan experiences.

- Ride lots of trains and subways.
- Visit a public bath.
- And more.

These are not listed in any order of priority, and I'm not saying we got to *do* all of these things. Studio Ghibli tickets, for instance, proved as difficult to obtain as front-row seats to a Taylor Swift concert. More on that later. I'm also not saying that all of our activities ended up worthwhile, but this was our list and it created a good way to start thinking about our trip.

One thing the list immediately told us is that we wanted to spend a significant portion of our time in Tokyo. In fact, I realized early on that we could spend the entire trip in Tokyo, and still have plenty left to do there. What you do and where, though, will also be shaped by the next step, deciding how much time you have to spend in the country. **(For some ideas on what to see and do, see our and Roy's lists of favorite things in "Part IX: Get Ready for Fun.")**

友 ROY RECOMMENDS

Attend a Festival

To our regret, one thing Tessa and I did not do in Japan was see a festival. Besides being fun, festivals give travelers key insights into Japanese culture. "We Japanese are very reserved," Roy explains, "but if you find Japanese people are 100% reserved, I have to say your observation is very superficial. We have fun. A lot of fun. We love sake, dances, fights, and festivals. Here is a reason why I strongly recommend that you join a festival once at least. Without knowing this side of Japanese culture, you can't understand why we are calm and disciplined on the surface." Festivals often feature floats, parades, and all manner of revelry. Roy's favorite festivals?

- NEBUTA MATSURI FESTIVAL IN AOMORI
- AWA SUMMER DANCE FESTIVAL
- GION MATSURI FESTIVAL IN KYOTO

My cousin Lisa spent several years teaching English in Kyoto, and like Roy, also strongly recommends attending a festival. Her favorites include the fire festival held each October in the mountain town of Kurama outside of Kyoto, and one that Roy also mentions, the famous Gion Matsuri festival, also in Kyoto and held each July. About the latter, Lisa adds, "It's easy to see—you just sit on a curb or a bit of grass anywhere and the parade eventually comes by, but honestly? I prefer the drumming and the shouting and the sake!" The Japan.travel website has further information on all of these festivals.

友 ROY RECOMMENDS

Read Up On Historical Sites

Knowing the history and background of places always adds satisfaction to a journey, and because Westerners know so little about it, this can be especially true of Japan. "Your visit will be much deeper and more meaningful if you know the history of the sites," Roy says. "For example, one of my favorite castles is the small, yet beautiful, Odawara Castle. Because it stands just several minutes' walk from Odawara's shinkansen station, the castle is especially popular for foreign travelers staying in Tokyo or Yokohama—but only a few people know how important this castle is in Japanese history. The castle is known as the first castle which was designed to GOVERN the people—not just fight against the enemy. The last battle around the castle is still legendary to this day."

STEP 2
DECIDE HOW MUCH TIME YOU WANT TO SPEND IN JAPAN

Although the overall cost of lodging, food, and travel in Japan is about on par with the U.S. or Europe, the cost and travel time involved with flying to Japan argues for a longer, rather than shorter, stay. Personally, I'd commit to a two-week minimum, but if, say, you have a line on cheap airfares, maybe a week will work for you. Tessa and I decided we needed *at least three weeks* to give us the kind of experience we craved, and for us that turned out to be about right. Let's dissect this further.

One-Week Considerations

If a week is all you've got for your trip, well, there's not much you can do about it. If that's the case, however, I personally would opt for a destination closer to home and wait until you have a longer period of time before visiting Japan. Why? For one, it'll probably take you a week to get over your jet lag. If you haven't experienced jet lag before, it means you'll be waking up at two in the morning and spending five or six hours waiting until you can begin your day—and that you'll

A mere one-week visit to Japan barely allows you to see the basic sights, such as the Imperial Palace grounds.

be ready for bed by three or four p.m. Yes, you can and should fight this by staying up as long as possible, but there's a good chance you'll be dragging yourself through your entire first week before your brain and body get in synch with Japan time. If your trip only lasts a week, well, that's going to suck.

Also keep in mind that you can spend one entire week just in Tokyo without batting a jet-lagged eyelash. Between museums, parks, shopping, eating, hitting public baths, and more, you'll feel like you've barely scratched the surface after seven days. You probably won't want to confine yourself to Tokyo, either. You'll perhaps want to take a day trip to Kyoto or Mt. Fuji during that week, leaving you even less time to soak up one of the world's most vibrant cities.

The only real advantage I can think of for spending a mere week in Japan is this: if you spend your week all in Tokyo, you probably won't need to buy a Japan Rail Pass. More on that in **"Part III: Using Japan's Transportation."**

Two-Week Considerations

For a first-time trip to Japan, two weeks is a viable option. Various sightseeing guides suggest different itineraries depending on how much time you have, and two weeks seems to be about average. In two weeks, you can spend a solid week in Tokyo, have three days in Kyoto and a day or two in Osaka–and still have time for a stop in one or two other places, such as Nara, Hiroshima, or the mountain town of Hakone. Two weeks also will allow you to recover from your jet lag, optimize the use of a JR Pass, and maybe take a "personal day" in case you feel exhausted, fall ill, or hit a bad patch of weather. In my opinion, though, two weeks will still leave you feeling rushed, which is why I strongly advocate for . . .

Three Weeks or Longer

With a stay of one or two weeks, let's face it, you are basically going to be pounding the tourist trail without much time to relax and soak up the essence of the country. And this raises the difference between a tourist and a traveler. Most people are tourists. They go places to see sights, eat what they're supposed to eat, do what they're supposed to do, and then go home. There's nothing wrong with this and I have done it myself. I just don't find it very satisfying.

A longer stay in Japan allows you to get off the beaten path a bit, such as visiting the charming castle city of Kanazawa.

I care less about sights than I do about experiencing the rhythm and flow of a place, trying out some of what the locals do, and hitting a few places tourists rarely visit. This approach isn't for everyone—and I'm not saying it's the *best* way to travel—but if that also is your style, I recommend stretching your trip to at least three weeks.

Three weeks allows you to do all the stuff you are supposed to do, while still experimenting with a few lesser-known options. Three weeks, for instance, allowed my daughter and me to visit both the seaside town of Kamakura and the "castle town" of Kanazawa, and they turned out to be two of our favorite places of the entire trip. These places are frequented by tourists, but not by many on a two-week schedule, and we wouldn't have visited them if we hadn't planned a longer trip. **(For our top 25 list of things we enjoyed, see "Part IX: Get Ready for Fun.")**

By having a more leisurely schedule, we also were able to shift gears one day when it looked like Tokyo might get hammered by rain. Instead of trudging around under umbrellas, we used our JR Passes to catch a shinkansen (bullet train) up to Sendai for the day. This city of a million holds few obvious tourist attractions, but we enjoyed it immensely. We ate food in a cool little corner diner that served only fifteen people at a time. We walked to a lovely park where I saw my first Japanese Pygmy Woodpecker. We also became friends with a charming woman at the tourist information office, who gave us travel tips and showed us where to buy kikufuku, a local delicacy. These are the kinds of experiences an extra week can get you, so if you have the option, I urge you to go for it.

友 *ROY RECOMMENDS*

Yokohama for Families

"If you are with your young kid(s)," Roy offers, "consider staying in Yokohama instead of Tokyo. Tokyo is such a fun place that you never get bored. It literally has everything, and something is happening every day. But if you are with young kids, it's another story, and actually many attractions, restaurants, shops, districts, and places in Tokyo are not good for young kids.

"Typically, for instance, young kids are not big fans of history or fashion. All they love is parks, gardens, open spaces and animals, so check what you can do with your kids in Yokohama. Downtown Yokohama is like one complete amusement park. It has everything for every generation."

SUGGESTIONS FOR FUN THINGS TO DO WITH YOUR KIDS IN YOKOHAMA:

Cup Noodles Museum

Yokohama Landmark Tower (second tallest in Japan)

Yokohama Cosmo World amusement park (Ferris wheel)

Red Brick Warehouse (shops and restaurants)

Gundam Factory Yokohama
(mecha toys and action figures; includes the moving Gundam)

Yamashita Park (with Yokohama Bay Bridge view)

Mega Don Quijote (large chain store popular for souvenir shopping)

Chinatown (the largest in Japan)

Motomachi shopping street

Sea bus (Yokohama Station to Yamashita Park)

Lunch/dinner cruise

Yokohama baseball stadium (Yokohama Baystars)

Osanbashi international pier

Nissan global headquarters

Yokohama Zoo zoorasia (open zoo, one hour by train/bus)

Yokohama Hakkeijima Sea Paradise (ocean animal park, one hour by train)

STEP 3
CHOOSE A SEASON TO VISIT AND BUY YOUR AIRLINE TICKETS

Unless you have a particular craving for bitter cold, or hot rain-soaked humidity, winter and summer probably will not be your top choices to visit Japan. I've never been in either season, but have experienced other Asian locations in summer and, well, you have to have a high tolerance for misery to enjoy it. Winter and summer *do* offer certain festivals and other events, and Japan does have some great skiing, but spring and fall are the overwhelming preferences of most first-time visitors—and for good reasons.

Spring offers both a respite from heavy rains and cold winter, and a chance to see one of Japan's most famous sights—the flowering sakura (cherry) trees that blanket much of the country. Fall offers similar conditions but with spectacular fall leaves.

As we were contemplating our trip, I felt game to try either season, but leaned toward fall after imagining a spring visit full of horrendous crowds. Spring, though, fit Tessa's school schedule better so we decided to go for it—and are happy we did. Not only did the pink and white blossoms of flowering trees add an almost mystical element to much of the country, we could not have asked for better weather. To top it off, the crowds stayed tolerable, even at the most popular shrines in Kyoto. About the only place swarms of people really killed us was Tokyo Disney, where lines of up to two-and-a-half hours prevented us from trying any of the top rides. That said, I'm guessing that fall offers a mellower, more contemplative season to visit, so whichever you prefer will be your best choice.

Once you've picked a season, it's time to take a deep breath and buy your airline tickets. Again, anything I say about prices will be dated by the time you read this, but generally expect to pay between one and two grand each for your tickets. Because I am a SkyMiles member, I chose to book our overseas flight with Delta Air Lines, and was very happy with that decision. If you're a risk-taker, you can roll the dice with a cut-rate, third-party airline ticket provider and possibly get seats for a lot cheaper, but I've heard enough horror stories about such "deals" that I choose to pay more and retain my peace of mind.

Roy agrees, stating, "Cheap air tickets come with cheap supports. In Japan, ANA and JAL are the most reliable airline companies. Even

Spring, the most favored travel season in Japan, can throw a few showers at you, but nothing that can't be handled with an umbrella and raincoat.

Thinking creatively about your route to Japan can help you save hundreds of dollars on flights.

though the tickets are not cheap, their support and hospitality are at the next level. I strongly recommend you choose ANA or JAL for your international flight, if you can. Your Japan experience will begin as soon as you check in at the ANA and JAL counters in the airport of your home country."

Whichever airline you choose, prices obviously will be cheaper from major hubs, and perhaps even cheaper from some West Coast locations. Flying from Missoula, Montana we were pretty much going to get skewered one way or another, but I did save us money and got us better flights by separately booking our tickets from Missoula to Seattle (with Alaska/Horizon), and from Seattle to Tokyo. Looking back, flying through Los Angeles would have saved us even more, which brings me to some additional tips when shopping for flights:

- Think creatively about where your actual flight to Tokyo leaves from. Don't assume, for instance, that just because Atlanta is your closest major airport it will have the cheapest airfares—or that because Seattle sits closest to Japan it will be your best choice. It may be well worth your while to first fly to New York or LAX, for example, and then on to Tokyo. Checking out ticket prices on a site such as **Google Flights** (Google.com/travel/flights/) can help you figure out your best options.
- If your search results yield outrageously inconvenient schedules, consider booking the different legs of your flights separately. When I search Missoula to Tokyo directly, for instance, the airlines often come up with crazy layovers and flight times. If I book from Missoula to Seattle separately from Seattle to Tokyo, as described above, I can end up with a much better schedule. **You just have to weigh the chances that your first leg might get delayed or canceled, and what that might mean for your flight to Tokyo.**
- Even if you have a narrow window in which to travel, always click the "flexible schedule" box when searching for your flights. A day or two shift either way can save you hundreds of dollars—something that may make you decide to take an extra day or three off work.
- While Travelocity, Priceline, and other services will sell you tickets, I find I have fewer problems if I book my flights directly

from the airlines' own websites. Flights I have tried to buy from one popular service have vaporized right in the middle of the booking process. In another case, I bought a ticket for my stepmother, and when she arrived at the airport they informed her that the flight didn't exist at all! This kind of thing has never happened when I am buying through a specific airline's website. Also, if you do have flight or scheduling problems during your trip, it's often easier to resolve it with the airline if you have purchased the ticket directly from them.

JAPAN AIRLINES TRAVEL PASS

As we were going to press, Roy alerted me to the fact that Japan Airlines has come up with its own explorer pass aimed at visitors who want to fly to various destinations within Japan. The service offers great fares on domestic flights to more than thirty cities, and if you'd rather fly than take a train to a distant city, it might be a good choice for you. Learn more at:

➤ *www.jal.co.jp/aul/en/world/japan_explorer_pass/lp/*

STEP 4
GET FAMILIAR WITH THE BASIC TRANSPORTATION SYSTEM

Normally, the next step would be to pick out where you want to stay and book your lodging. Before doing that, however, it's worth a sneak preview into Japan's remarkable transportation system. Why? Because a quick look will prove helpful in selecting your accommodations in each place you visit. **(Again, I'll cover transportation in detail in "Part III: Using Japan's Transportation.")**

Like most places, Japan has a mix of cars, taxis, buses, bicycles, and even scooters available to the savvy traveler. What really sets Japan apart from most other nations, though, is its abundance of trains! For those of you familiar with the *Thomas the Tank Engine* books or television series, well, Japan really is the island of Sodor! And that's a great thing, especially for the first-time traveler, because Japan's trains are reasonably priced and they're enormously convenient.

Trains provide easy, comfortable ways to get between cities. They provide excellent transportation *within* most bigger cities, too. You are undoubtedly familiar with the country's famous bullet trains, or shinkansen, but many other excellent rail lines connect cities throughout the country. Just as wonderful, at least ten metropolitan areas boast extensive subway and other urban rail systems. In a place such as Tokyo, figuring out the subway system can at first seem daunting, but trust me, you will quickly master it.

The point here is that Japan's trains allow you to travel the country virtually car-free—and you will want to pick out hotels that are easy walking distances to some kind of rail or subway station. How? **Google Maps** (Google.com/maps) is an invaluable tool in figuring this out. Let's say you want to stay at Hotel A in Kyoto, but aren't sure how far of a walk it is from the nearest subway station. Simply do the following:

1) Call up Google Maps and type in "Kyoto Station" (the place you most likely will be arriving when you first get to Kyoto).
2) Once Kyoto Station appears on screen, click "Directions." Then, swap the starting point and destination by clicking on the little up and down arrow icon so that your trip *begins* at Kyoto Station.

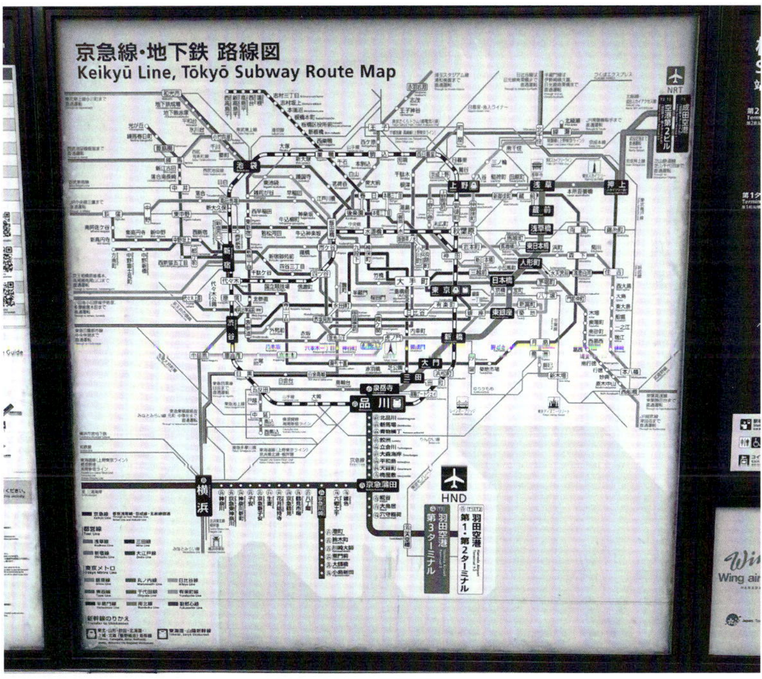

Getting a rough understanding of the urban transportation systems before you book your accommodations can save you time, stress, and money later.

3) Type in Hotel A as the destination, and make sure the little public transportation icon is selected for how you want to travel.

4) Various options will appear for travel during the next hour or so. Click the Details for one of them to see the step-by-step moves for how to make that journey. The final step will indicate how far you'll have to walk from your *last* train or subway stop to the hotel.

Since Japan is many hours ahead of you, you can get a more accurate result by manually changing your departure time to a typical daylight hour and then running the search again.

Google may inform you that one or more steps in your travel involve taking a bus, and if so, it will show you the details you need to know. Buses, it turns out, are almost as easy to negotiate in Japan as the trains (more on that later), but for your first trip, if a bus is required, you might want to consider a different hotel option so that you can stick to trains and subways.

The bottom line is that I ran this kind of check before booking every hotel, and it made the entire booking process remarkably easy. And with that knowledge in mind, it's on to . . .

STEP 5
GROUP YOUR ACTIVITIES BY LOCATION AND BOOK ACCOMMODATIONS

Although I cover it here in one step, booking your accommodations actually requires a couple of different phases. The first is deciding which area, or areas, you wish to stay, especially in large cities. The second is choosing your specific accommodations and making reservations. Let's consider them one at a time.

Choosing the Areas or Neighborhoods You Wish to Stay

It may seem like an obvious strategy to book your lodging close to things that you want to do or see, but in a place like Tokyo or Osaka this can require extra analysis. After you've done your research on what you want to do in Tokyo, Kyoto, and other cities, again jump on Google Maps to get a visual on where each activity is located. Tokyo especially is a vast city and just because two things are located "in Tokyo" doesn't mean they are close together or easily reachable from anywhere. For Tokyo, in fact, I highly recommend picking two *separate* areas to stay during your visit, and enjoy your activities accordingly.

For our trip, we spent five nights in Tokyo on the front end of the trip and four more nights on the back end. That gave us a great opportunity to stay in two different parts of the city. For our first location, we chose a hotel across from Tokyo Station, which is located near Ginza, the Tsukiji Outer Market, Tokyo Tower, Akihabara, Tokyo Dome, Ueno Park, and a number of the city's best museums. Tokyo Station also offers a direct train to Tokyo Disney, so naturally we focused on these activities during our first stint in Tokyo.

For our second stay in Tokyo, we chose a hotel near the more swinging center of Shibuya. There, we focused our time on shopping, seeing some great city parks, paying our respects at the Hachiko memorial, and visiting the observatory atop the Tokyo Metropolitan Government Building. We would have also visited Studio Ghibli from this side of town–if we had managed to score tickets.

You may think this focus on locations isn't a big deal, but the most direct route across town from Shibuya to Tokyo Station takes around 20 minutes–40 round-trip–and usually longer. Do you want to spend that extra time in a packed subway, or doing something fun? If you have the time, a "two locations" strategy easily can end up saving you an hour or more a day, something your tired legs and feet will appreciate.

Even our lowest-priced budget hotel room proved clean and comfortable.

For other cities, two locations probably isn't so important. In Kyoto, we picked a place that was about ten minutes' walk to Nishiki Market, the Kamo River, and two different subway lines. This allowed us to reach everywhere we wanted to go with only modest effort. Still, if you especially want to hit Kiyomizu-dera Temple and other temples and shrines on the east side of town, think about booking a place that puts you within easy walking distance of at least a couple of them.

友 *ROY RECOMMENDS*

Stuck Without a Room, or Swimming in Luxury

In the unlikely event that you somehow find yourself without a room one night, or are on an extreme budget, don't despair. Bigger cities especially have "emergency options" that will get you through the night. Roy suggests the following:

- Renting a karaoke room
- Renting a small room in an internet café
- Hanging out in a manga kissa (manga café, similar to internet café)
- Visiting a super sento (public bathhouse, with reclining seats or private rooms)
- Visiting a sauna (similar system as super sento)
- Hitting the late show in a cinema (an old school choice)

These options range from about 2,000 to 5,000 yen per night, but will keep you out of the cold—and maybe even let you catch some shut-eye.

At the other extreme, if you have the means for a real splurge, the Tokyo Station Hotel sits at the top of Roy's list. "In so many ways, no hotel can beat this breathtakingly beautiful yet heartwarming hotel," he opines. "The experience is like being invited to this country as a State Guest." He also recommends these other special, one-of-a-kind hotels:

NIKKO KANAYA HOTEL, NIKKO (near Nikko National Park)

FUJIYA HOTEL, HAKONE

MANPEI HOTEL, KARUIZAWA

NARA HOTEL, NARA

HOTEL NEW GRAND, YOKOHAMA

GAMAGORI CLASSIC HOTEL, GAMAGORI (near Nagoya)

UNZEN KANKO HOTEL (Unzen-Amakusa National Park, near Nagasaki)

KAWANA HOTEL (South of Hakone)

KAMIKOCHI IMPERIAL HOTEL (Chubu-Sangaku National Park)

"If you are a guy who think it's crazy to splurge just for a bed," he adds, "please drop in at these hotels for a cup of coffee. You may soon recognize the classic and serene vibe which only tradition can give."

Selecting Your Accommodations and Reserving Your Rooms

When it comes to actually booking your accommodations, you have oodles of options. I used to always go directly through an individual hotel's–or hotel chain's–website. Then, I became a fan of Booking.com. Unlike certain other online booking services, I never had a single problem using this site, and it allowed me to reserve hotels for our entire Japan trip in a flash. The problem? As we were going to press, multiple reports began emerging that Booking.com was dragging its feet on paying the hotels it listed–a practice none of us should support, so please check for updates on this situation. If you do use a booking site such as this, be sure you pay attention to a few things:

- The rating a hotel is given on the site you're using.
- The last penalty-free date you are allowed to cancel or modify your booking.
- Whether a place offers a complimentary breakfast.
- If they offer a shuttle from the nearest train station or airport.
- And again, how close the hotel is to subway and train stations **(see previous chapter)**.

In Japan, we found that independent hotels and certain Japanese hotel chains are cheaper and offer better value than big Western chains. You also can save money by booking many months–or even a year–ahead of time. This is especially true if you intend to travel during a high-tourist season such as "sakura season" or Golden Week, when a bunch of tightly-packed holidays lead to heavy travel within the country.

Roy adds that, typically, Japan hotel rates shift through three phases:

1) Early reservation discount rate

2) Normal list rate

3) Last minute dirt cheap price rate

"Of course, choice 1 is recommended," he says, "while choice 3 is too risky. If you wait too long to book, you will probably have to choose the most expensive room in a region, or successfully find a room that is dirt cheap."

Here are some solid hotel chains Roy suggests checking out:

APA Hotels & Resorts

Sotetsu Fresa Inn

Hotel Route Inn

Toyoko Inn (not a misspelling)

Super Hotel

Daiwa Roynet

Tokyu Rei hotel

Tokyu Stay

Hotel Dormy Inn

Richmond Hotel

He also recommends the following hotels in Tokyo:

Akihabara Washington Hotel (great location next to the subway station)

Hilltop Hotel (quiet and cozy)

Hotel Grand Arc Hanzomon (next to the Imperial Palace)

Palace Hotel Tokyo (next to the Imperial Palace)

I'll add that Tessa and I stayed in seven different places in Japan, all of them in what I consider a modest or medium price range. Most were independently operated but two belonged to Japanese hotel chains (including the Sotetsu Fresa chain), and we were extremely satisfied by all of them. Each of our accommodations was clean, quiet, and well-appointed. Each also offered a better value than a similarly-priced hotel in the U.S. or, I presume, the more popular European destinations. My point: don't be afraid to try something just because you've never heard of it. If it has a decent rating–for instance, in the 7s or above on Booking.com, or 3.8 or above on Google–you will probably be happy with it. We were.

For more information on booking your lodging, see "Japan Book & Website Travel Resources" at the end of this book.

TRAVELING WITH FAMILIES

One problem I have encountered traveling in Asia and elsewhere is that most rooms are designed specifically for solo travelers or couples. This makes finding a room that can accommodate a family with kids a special challenge. The demand for such accommodations has given rise to the "apartment hotel" concept in Japan. These locations provide more space and more beds for larger groups of people. To learn more, Roy suggests looking up the Mimaru chain website:

➤ *www.mimaruhotels.com/en/*

Additional Hotel/Transportation Considerations

How do you choose your hotels in cities?" Roy asks. "The answer is simple: Find hotels as close to train stations as possible—preferably a major hub station."

"After being overwhelmed by the subway map of Tokyo," Roy continues, "many travelers try to find another transportation option. Some consider renting a car, but driving a car in big cities is not just stressful but also extremely dangerous, especially if you are from a country that drives on the right-hand side of the road. Additionally, it may take you 30 minutes just to find a parking lot—which is still a long walk from the place you want to visit. The bottom line is that nothing can beat Japanese public transportation systems, especially in cities.

"Because of this, the distance between the nearest train station and your hotel matters very much. And if your hotel is only one or two minutes away from a major hub station, you don't even need to worry about the rain, because many facilities are connected by an underground network of passageways in big cities.

"Please keep in mind that some stations are so huge that the nearest hotels from these stations actually require a ten-minute walk from the *train platforms* (e.g. Shinjuku, Shibuya, and Ikebukuro). On the other hand, some major hub stations have accommodations that are very close (e.g. Tokyo, Shinbashi, and Shinagawa). If your main interest is to check the latest fashions on the streets of Shibuya, for example, consider a business hotel in Shinbashi, which stands only a five-minute walk from the train platforms. This will allow you to hop the Yamanote JR train for a quick ride up to Shibuya."

Roy adds that in Tokyo, shinkansens stop at Tokyo, Ueno, and Shinagawa stations so choosing hotels around one of these stations can be a huge advantage.

He has one more recommendation for people with late arrivals. "If you are a budget traveler and your flight is arriving at the airport late night," he advises, "please stay at a hotel in the airport. There are so-called 'capsule hotels'[3] in Narita, Haneda, and Kansai airports and they are much more spacious than you think. Every capsule and the public space are so clean that this will definitely be your first authentic Japanese experience!" Nine Hours (ninehours.co.jp/) and First Cabin (en.first-cabin.jp/) are two highly-recommended capsule hotel chains, but don't be afraid to consider other capsule hotels, too.

---

[3] Capsule, or "pod," hotels offer a kind of "cubby" or "tube" instead of a full room. They have shared bathrooms and other facilities, but most are very clean and comfortable. They are especially great for solo travelers on a budget.

STEP 6
RESERVE TICKETS FOR SPECIALIZED EVENTS AND SIGHTS

This step goes hand-in-hand with steps 1 and 3, so you may actually want to look into it earlier in your Japan Game Plan process—especially if you have flexibility in the dates and time of year you want to visit. For instance, if you really want to see a sumo wrestling match, you need to know that there are only six big tournaments a year and if you're not in the country when they occur, well, you're out of luck. On the other hand, if you are planning at least a few months in advance, you probably will have time to book most events that can sell out quickly. Besides sumo, a few examples include visiting or attending:

- Studio Ghibli
- A professional baseball game
- Tokyo Disney

All four of the above things were on our list of things to do, and we only partly succeeded in doing them. The Osaka sumo tournament was wrapping up while we were still in Tokyo and Kamakura, for instance, so we couldn't attend a day of matches. That actually turned out to be a bit of a blessing because it aired nightly on television. Jet-lagged and exhausted from each day, we watched the nightly broadcast in the comfort of our room, and it proved a wonderful way to recover during the evenings. We also got to see far more matches and get to know more of the wrestlers than if we'd attended live.

Getting Studio Ghibli tickets, on the other hand, turned into a bust. At the time of our trip, tickets to this popular attraction went on sale on a particular day the month *before* you wanted to visit, and I sat poised and ready to go on the website the moment sales began. Unfortunately, so many people were trying to do the same thing that the system locked up again and again. By the time I broke through, the tickets had vanished, and there was nothing I could do about it. Hopefully, you'll have better luck, but be sure to check their website many months in advance so you understand your best approach to scoring a spot.

Ditto with Tokyo Disney. For mysterious reasons, their website wouldn't let me buy tickets ahead of time, so we chose to just show up there in person. We *were* able to buy tickets, but by mid-day the

Although temples and shrines such as Kyoto's Fushimi Inari Taisha shrine don't require reservations, getting there early can ensure a more pleasant, less crowded experience.

lines were so long—think two hours and more for the coaster rides—that we were relegated to the less popular attractions. I will say that Disney Sea was especially wonderful in its concept and layout, but get there early or stay late if you want a crack at the Raging Spirits or Journey to the Center of the Earth rollercoasters. To avoid the worst crowds, Roy also recommends checking Japan's holiday and school schedules ahead of time to make sure you don't plan to go on an especially busy day.

Our best "special events" luck came with seeing a Nippon Professional Baseball league game. Getting online a few weeks before our visit, I was able to purchase great seats along the third base line for a game between the Yomiuri ("Tokyo") Giants and the Yokohama

DeNA BayStars. The Giants are similar to the Yankees in that they've won far more than their share of championships, and are hated by everyone except their own supporters. The Yokohama fans, however, out-cheered the Giants fans, leading to a 1-0 Yokohama victory. Even if you aren't a die-hard baseball fan (and we aren't), these games are huge fun, and give you a chance to see the Japanese really cut loose and go crazy. Seeing the game proved to be one of our favorite Japan experiences. **For more information on any of the above events, consult the web links listed in "Japan Book & Website Travel Resources" at the end of this book.**

Besides attractions like those above, you'll again want to research specific festivals or tours you want to attend or do. As indicated before, a ton of festivals take place throughout Japan and at all times of the year. If there's one that's especially important to you, it will pay to find out the details and make appropriate reservations as far as possible ahead of time. Although a festival itself may not require reservations, hotels may fill up so you'll want to book one right away.

One more note: in our experience, shrines and temples don't require advance reservations to visit, but some such as Kyoto's Fushimi Inari Taisha shrine, with its thousands of red gates, can get quite crowded. Plan on hitting these places early in the day.

STEP 7
CREATE A DETAILED ITINERARY

Okay, so finally you know where you want to go in Japan and when. You've bought your airline tickets and booked your hotels. You have your documents and finances lined up. For your next planning step, I highly recommend creating a detailed, day-by-day itinerary for your trip.

You don't need to type out an itinerary, of course, but here are some compelling reasons to do so:

- It will help you spot anything you've overlooked ahead of time, such as a night you failed to book a hotel or whether you've miscalculated the date you will need to order your rail pass **(see "Step 8: Buy Your Japan Rail Pass Vouchers")**.
- It will help you "anchor" your entire trip into your brain, reducing anxiety and allowing you to relax and look forward to your adventure.

- It will help you refine your plans and make them more efficient—and also add other activities you may have overlooked earlier.
- **In Japan especially, placing transportation details on a piece of paper will save you both confusion and frustration.**

To illustrate the last important point, here is my itinerary for the day we traveled from the seaside town of Kamakura to Kyoto:

Monday, March 27

- Travel to Kyoto.

  From Kamakura, take the Shonan-Shinjuku or Yokosuka train North to Ofuna Station. From there take the Tokaido Line to Odawara Station. From there, take the Tokaido-Sanyo shinkansen to Kyoto.
- Could also take the Yokosuka Line (Local Narita Airport) to Shinagawa Station and then pick up the same shinkansen there.
- **Upon arrival in Kyoto, buy the Kansai One Pass at Kyoto Station to ride all trains in the area.**
- Stay at (I included hotel address, phone, and reservation # here). Take the Karasuma Line North to Shijo Station and then walk to our place from there. (Breakfast $9 each if sign up.)
- Eat at Nishiki Market (8 minute walk north from our place)—and walk through Gion if we feel like it.

You'll see that in this entry, I especially included a lot of details about just how we were going to get from one place to another, and I have a confession to make: to get to Odawara Station to catch the shinkansen to Kyoto, we actually took a different route than any I listed above.[4] Just writing out the possibilities ahead of time, though, helped me understand the available options and allowed me to feel much more comfortable about what we needed to do.

Where this entry *really* saved us anxiety, though, was the second-to-last line, "Take the Karasuma Line North to Shijo Station and then walk to our place from there." Why? Well, unlike Tokyo Station, which we found easy to negotiate, Kyoto Station proved to be much more of a madhouse. I had *intended* to buy the Kansai One Pass there to ride the subways, but the station was so confusing and overwhelming

[4] We ended up riding the Enoshima Electric Railway to Fujisawa Station, where we picked up the JR Tokaido Line to Odawara, and took the shinkansen from there.

after our already-long day of travel, it looked like it would be a major chore to figure out *where* to buy the pass. In short, we just wanted to get out of there!

Fortunately, I had written down which subway to take, so we were prepared. Tessa spotted a sign for the Karasuma subway line and we made a bee-line for it. To board the subway, we simply pulled out the pre-paid IC cards that we'd bought earlier **(see "Trains: A Quick Overview" in Part III)**, hopped on the first train, and five minutes later got off at the stop nearest our hotel. I'm not exaggerating when I say this one detail pretty much saved my sanity for the afternoon. Oh, and it turns out that the Kansai One Pass wouldn't have saved us any money anyway!

This example brings up another important point: *there's no need to slavishly follow your itinerary*. Once you're in Japan, you'll receive new information almost daily that will lead you to revise what you want to do and how. Having everything printed out and organized in ways that make sense allows you to easily switch things up on the fly. In fact, we rarely visited sights on the days that we had them listed on our itinerary, but knowing which places lay close together helped us choose what to do and when.

A detailed itinerary can help you quickly escape the craziness at places such as Kyoto Station.

Here are a couple of other itinerary tips:

- Try to format your itinerary by location, e.g. a page for Tokyo, a page for Kyoto, etc . . . Print out an extra copy so that when you reach a new location you can just tear off the appropriate page and shove it into your pocket. This will give you easy access to it without having to dig into your daypack or purse, or search for it on your phone.
- Speaking of phones, send a copy of your itinerary to your phone and store it in your "Files" folder or app. That way, if you lose all of your printed copies, it will still be at your fingertips. You should store a copy somewhere on the cloud (e.g. Google Drive) for the same reason.
- Include a variety of things you'd like to do in a place in case your top choice or choices don't work out. For Kanazawa, for instance, I included the following list:

  Things to do in Kanazawa

  - Kenrokuen Garden
  - Higashichaya Old Town (Higashi Chaya District), 10 minutes NNE across the river
  - **Old Teahouse street**–just along the river on way to above Old Town
  - Kaikaro Teahouse (in the Higashichaya Old Town)
  - Omicho Market, NW of the castle park near us, probably 10 minutes
  - Big Castle
  - **Bird Kenmin Seaside Park** (Walk west to Minami-cho/Oyama Jinja Shrine; get Bus 34/63 and ride to the end; there walk south across the river to the park–allow about an hour total transit)

We didn't do all of these things–but it was nice to know we had additional, fun options if opportunities arose, or something else didn't work out. Roy adds, "Some people say you should not make too long of a 'to do list,' because you can't do it all anyway. That's true, but making a long list won't hurt. One of the best parts of a trip is that you feel like you are traveling while you are doing your planning. I always make a long, long wish list, and choose two or three 'must-see places' on it. After all, you are not sure how you will be feeling and what will be happening until you get there. Sometimes, for instance, your interest may completely disappear when you see a long queue in front of a planned place. That's the time to check your abundantly long list. The more alternatives you have, the more you can improvise."

You'll discern that I just typed our itinerary into a word-processing document, but as you might expect, there are apps that can help you do this, too. If these interest you, just run an internet search on itinerary planning apps. **For a basic outline of our own Japan itinerary, see "Part IX: Get Ready for Fun."**

STEP 8
BUY YOUR JAPAN RAIL PASS VOUCHERS—IF YOU NEED THEM

With your itinerary in hand, the final big step in your planning process is to buy your Japan Rail Pass vouchers. Note that I didn't say buy your *Japan Rail Passes*. That's because you can't get your actual passes until you arrive in Japan. Instead, you will purchase vouchers to take with you to Japan, and then exchange them for your passes at a Japan Railways office once you get there **(see Part III for more details on this exchange)**.

Before you do purchase a voucher, though, it's worth devoting a few words to whether you should obtain a JR Pass at all. At the time Tessa and I visited Japan, the Japan Rail Pass was hands-down a great deal for foreign visitors. At the end of 2023, however, JR imposed a significant hike on prices, meaning you need to give more consideration to whether you really should buy one or not. "From 2024 onward," Roy elaborates, "the JR Pass is no longer a magic wand. Unless you are visiting multiple cities by shinkansen in a limited time, you hardly exceed the break-even point." We recommend that you use Google Maps to calculate the cost of the shinkansen or other long-distance trains you plan to take during your visit, and add them up to see if buying a JR Pass makes sense.

If you do decide that a pass makes sense, purchasing the Japan Rail Pass vouchers is incredibly easy—as long as you do it at least two or three weeks before your departure. Here's how:

- Go to the **Japan Rail Pass** website, which at the time of this writing, is at:
  - ➤ **www.japanrailpass.net/en/**
- Click on the "Purchase" icon in the top menu bar.
- Follow the instructions under "Purchase Online" option.

You *will* need to create an account to purchase the vouchers. At the time of your purchase, you also can make reservations for specific trains–but you do not *need* to do this. We waited until we reached Japan to reserve various train rides. This was easy to do both at JR offices and at ticket machines in various stations. Many local and intercity JR trains do not require or even take reservations–but we went ahead and reserved seats for any especially important trips or those that might be crowded. More on that in Part III.

In any case, once you make your purchase, the physical vouchers are mailed to you–which is why you want to make sure you order them at least a few weeks ahead of time in case there are problems. And now, the most important thing . . . ***You must take these physical vouchers with you to Japan and present them with your passports to obtain your actual rail passes.***

Note that foreign visitors *can* buy JR Passes once they arrive in Japan–but they will cost a bit more. Whether you purchase vouchers ahead of time or passes in Japan, you will need to decide three things at the time of your purchase . . .

1. Which JR Region to Purchase

Japan Railways is actually a consortium of six different companies: JR East, JR West, JR Central, JR Shikoku, JR Kyushu, and JR Hokkaido. These companies each control a different region of the country. And while you can buy slightly cheaper passes just for a specific region of coverage, your savings won't be that great *and* it will give you far less flexibility in your trip. In short, **you will most likely want to buy the overall JR Pass that covers the entire country**–at least for your first visit to Japan. The exception might be if you know you will be staying in only one area, such as Tokyo, in which case you will want to look up JR Pass options just for that area at:

➤ **www.jrpass.com/regional-passes**

2. First or Regular Class?

Once you start the purchasing process, you'll also see that you can buy either a **Green** ("business class") pass or an **Ordinary** (regular) pass. We bought the Ordinary pass and were perfectly pleased with it. We also saved about 25% by doing so.

3. Duration of Your Pass

The third thing you'll have to decide is if you want to buy your pass for one, two, or three weeks. Since our trip was going to last three weeks, I naturally assumed we would need three-week passes—but one benefit of writing out our itinerary is that it made me recognize that we would be spending a full nine or ten days in Tokyo. While JR does run important trains in and around Tokyo, a JR Pass can be less useful there, and not as cost efficient. As a result, we were able to save money by buying two-week passes, and employing the following strategy:

- Upon our arrival in Tokyo, using a three-day subway pass (about $15) for our first few days there **(see Part III)**.
- Activating our JR Pass for the following two weeks, both for travel on JR trains within Tokyo (for a day or two) and, more importantly, for travel to Kamakura, Kyoto, Kanazawa, and other distant Japanese cities.
- Upon our return to Tokyo, using another subway pass or a prepaid IC (Suica or Pasmo) card to fill in our final days there **(see Part III)**.

If this sounds a bit confusing, it will become much clearer after you read the following chapters on transportation. **The point now is to think about how long you will be in major cities at the front and/ or tail ends of your trip, and whether you really need a JR Pass for those portions of your trip**. If you can get away with it, buying a shorter-duration pass could save you hundreds of dollars, especially because as I mentioned earlier, JR recently hiked the prices on their passes considerably. They are still a good value for many, but if you don't need a full three- or two-week pass, that's useful to know ahead of time.

With that, let's get into the nitty-gritty of understanding and using Japan's incredible transportation.

One choice you will make when purchasing your JR Pass voucher is whether to buy a Green or Ordinary pass. We found the Ordinary pass seats perfectly clean, spacious, and comfortable.

友 ROY RECOMMENDS

Beware of "Pass Traps"

Although many different places and organizations offer transportation and entry passes, they don't always end up being cost effective. "There are many kinds of passes all over Japan," Roy explains. "The Hakone Free Pass, for example, allows you to ride all of the transportation options in the Hakone area and gives you admission to selected tourist attractions. While these passes are beneficial for their specific purpose, there are also some limitations with them. In big cities like Tokyo, for instance, none of the passes covers *all* of the transportation systems. Roughly one-third of train systems are JR lines, another third are non-JR lines, and the rest are subways. In other words, if you keep trying to make the most of your pass, you often cannot travel efficiently from A to B, slowing you down and making you stressed out." To solve this problem, Roy recommends avoiding unnecessary passes, and when passes are not the most efficient option, using the IC cards we will explore in depth in the next section.

Tokyo Station has a dizzying network of train lines coming in and out of it including the famous shinkansen, or bullet trains.

PART III

Using Japan's Transportation

Trains: A Quick Overview

I've already provided some basics into Japan's remarkable transportation system, and now it's time to get into more detail about the type of transportation you will use on the vast majority of your travel: trains.

In Japan, you will be riding three major kinds of rail systems:

- **Subway systems** in large cities. In Tokyo these include both Tokyo Metro and Toei subway networks.
- **Japan Railways (JR) trains** within major cities and, crucially, *between* cities. These include both traditional trains and *shinkansen*, or bullet trains.
- **Systems run by independent operators** in various places. These include classic trains, monorails, cable cars, streetcars (trams), narrow gauge railways, and so forth.

All of these types of systems work wonderfully well, but they require slightly different ways of reserving and buying tickets. Before plunging into the details in the next chapters, here is the basic skinny . . .

- To ride subways, you will want to have either a subway pass or what is called an **IC card (integrated circuit card)**—basically a pre-paid credit card that can be repeatedly recharged with varying amounts of money (see sidebar).
- To ride Japan Railways (JR) trains, you will either use your JR Pass or, for local trips *before* you activate your JR Pass, pay for individual rides. You can pay for these individual rides either by tapping your IC card on entry and exit gates (short trips), or by purchasing tickets from machines or JR ticket windows (longer intercity trips).
- To ride trains run by independent operators, you also will use your IC card or you will buy individual tickets from machines or ticket windows.

To help you feel more comfortable with all this, let's walk through, step by step, how to get to your first hotel from your two most likely Japan entry points: Haneda and Narita airports. From either airport you have many, many transport options including taxis, buses, subways, and various trains. Unfortunately, this vast number of choices probably makes you feel more anxious, not less. The good news?

Each airport offers a couple of transportation options that stand out for their convenience and ease of use, and in the following two chapters I will focus on these. **Be sure to read both chapters to fully understand your options and what to do.**

ALL ABOUT IC CARDS

At least ten major brands of IC cards are sold in different parts of the country and they can be used interchangeably. The two dominant IC cards are the Suica and Pasmo cards popular in and around Tokyo. IC cards are sold at specified self-serve machines in almost any subway or train station, as well as at certain convenience stores and other outlets. IC cards can also be loaded onto your phones as apps. In most cases, you can use your IC card just by tapping it on a large pad on the station entry gate, and then tapping it again when you exit at another station. The cost of your ride will be automatically deducted from the card. Note: that you can only recharge IC cards at machines using cash, not credit cards. Learn more about IC cards at:

➤ **www.japan-guide.com/e/e2359_003.html**

IC cards such as the Suica and Pasmo cards offer incredibly convenient ways of paying for rail and bus transportation in Japan.

Not only is Haneda Airport Japan's busiest, it offers extremely easy rail-based options for getting into Tokyo.

Arriving at Haneda Airport
STEP BY STEP

Haneda Airport is Japan's busiest airport and, conveniently, sits less than an hour from most locations in Tokyo. The two transportation options below are incredibly easy and affordable, and will get you into the city in a flash. In most cases, they also should quickly deliver you close to your hotel, no matter which part of the city you are staying in.

HANEDA OPTION 1

Take the monorail from the airport and transfer to a train or subway.

Many travelers prefer this option as it is extremely simple and can be accomplished using your JR Pass, a Suica (IC) card, or regular ticket. Here's what to do:

Step 1 (optional): Leaving immigration, decide if you are going to exchange your JR Pass voucher for your JR Pass. If so, do that at the JR airport ticket office.

Step 2: Look for the overhead signs to the monorail (which are easily visible) and follow them to the gates.

Step 3: At the ticket machines next to the gates,

a) pull out your JR Pass OR

b) buy a Suica (IC) card loaded with a couple thousand yen OR

c) buy a ticket that will allow you to get to a specific destination in Tokyo using both the monorail and a connecting JR train.

Since you will probably want a Suica card for later use anyway, I recommend just buying and, if needed, using it here.

Step 4: Use your JR Pass, Suica card, or ticket to pass through the gate and board the monorail.[5]

Step 5: Ride the monorail about 13 minutes to Hamamatsuchō Station. Get off and exit the gate (turnstile) using your JR Pass, Suica card, or ticket.

Step 6: Follow overhead signs and/or the green signs painted on the floor to the JR trains.

Step 7: Ride either the JR Yamanote Line (JY) train or the JR Keihin-Tohoku Line (JK) train to your desired destination.

Step 8 (if necessary): If the JR train doesn't get you all the way to where you need to go, use your Suica card to transfer to the subway system at any transfer station, and ride the subway to the station that gets you closest to your hotel. (Note that if you don't need a JR train at all, you can exit at Hamamatsucho Station and walk about 300 yards to Daimon Station and pick up the subway there.)

An awesome video by ONE GOOD DREAM showing much of the above procedure can be found at:

➤ **www.youtube.com/watch?v=2ctgeiayE8k**

Extensive information about the monorail also can be found at:

➤ **www.tokyo-monorail.co.jp/english/**

---

[5] Again, if you have never used an IC (Suica, Pasmo, etc . . .) card, you simply tap the card on a large pad on the gate (or turnstile) to enter and exit different stations. When you exit, the amount of your fare is automatically deducted from the amount on the card. If you are using a ticket or JR Pass, you insert it into a slot instead of tapping it. It pops back up on top of the gate, where you collect it. Note, you need the ticket or pass both to enter and exit a station, so keep it in a safe place.

A typical train station "turnstile" showing the oval button for tapping an IC card and the slot below it for inserting your Japan Rail Pass or regular train ticket.

HANEDA OPTION 2

Take a train directly from the airport and transfer to another train and/or subway.

Tessa and I chose this second, excellent option from Haneda. It entailed riding an airport train directly from Haneda and then transferring to either a JR train or, in our case, to the subway system to get close to our hotel. Here's how to do it:

Step One: Leaving immigration from Terminal 3, **find the Keikyu Tourist Information Center** (www.haneda-tokyo-access.com/en/tic.html). This is located very close to where you leave immigration and customs–and right before the escalators that lead down to the train platform.

Step Two: At the information center, purchase a ticket that allows you to ride the Keikyu Airport Train toward Tokyo. At the same time, if you plan on using the subway system, purchase a "Welcome! Tokyo Subway Ticket" pass good for 24, 48, or 72 hours (depending on how long you plan to stay in Tokyo on arrival).

Step Three: Use your new Keikyu Airport Train ticket to go through the entry gates, and ride the escalator down to the Keikyu Airport Train platform.

Step Four: Board the Keikyu train toward Shinagawa/Narita Airport (not toward Yokohama) and ride it to Shinagawa Station.

Once you arrive at Shinagawa station, you have two choices.

***Choice 1:* Remain on the airport train to Sengakuji Station, and join the Tokyo subway system.**

If you plan to wait a day or more to activate your JR Pass and want to use your new "Welcome Tokyo" subway pass instead, **don't get off the airport train at Shinagawa Station with everyone else**. Instead, ride the Keikyu Airport Train one more stop to Sengakuji Station and get off there. Then, without changing platforms or going through any gates, catch a subway train of the Asakusa Line. This subway line will allow you to connect with the entire Tokyo subway system. From Sengakuji Station, for example, Tessa and I rode the subway to Nihombashi Station, which was close to our hotel–but you can ride it to any other station on the Asakusa Line. If you want to go to Tokyo Station, for example, ride the Asakusa Line subway to Shimbashi Station, and transfer to the Ueno-Tokyo Line. **Note that wherever you get off the subway *for the first time*, you will have to ask an agent there to validate your "Welcome! Tokyo" subway pass so you can exit the station and continue using your pass on other subway lines.**

***Choice 2:* Get off the Keikyu Airport Train at Shinagawa Station, and transfer to a JR train to reach your destination.**

As mentioned before, Japan Railways runs trains both within cities and between cities. This includes at least 15 different lines in and around Tokyo. In other words you can get to most parts of the city using *only* JR trains. However, to do this, you will either have to pay for individual train rides (preferably with an IC card) or exchange your Japan Rail Pass voucher for your actual Japan Rail Pass and activate it. How?

You can exchange your voucher at the JR ticket office at Haneda Airport or at the JR ticket office at Shinagawa Station–but be prepared for long lines. **In fact, one of the best reasons to stick to the subway (Choice 1 above) on your first day or two is so you don't have to wait in a long line to exchange your JR Pass voucher**. Instead, you can use the subway to get to your hotel and, the next day or later, exchange your voucher at a JR office in another station. We waited until the day after our arrival to exchange our vouchers, and did so at a JR office in Tokyo Station. Lines were short, and the person at the ticket window also helped us make a couple of train reservations we would need later. Other places around Tokyo to exchange your JR vouchers for your JR Passes include the Japan Railways offices at Narita Airport and at Ueno, Shinjuku, and Shibuya stations. A complete list can be found at:

➤ **japanrailpass.net/en/exchange.html**

友 *ROY RECOMMENDS*

Airport Limousine Buses for the Less Adventurous

If you are a first-timer to Japan, and not up for using public transportation, Roy suggests choosing an airport limousine bus to take you from the airport directly to your hotel, or at least close by. Airport limo buses run to dozens of locations throughout Tokyo and beyond, and are very reasonably priced (from Haneda, about $10 compared to around $100 for a taxi; from Narita, about $25 compared to around $250 for a taxi). If the bus doesn't take you within close walking distance to your hotel, a taxi is a good option for the final kilometer or two. "It will be much, much cheaper than taking the taxi all the way from the airport," Roy emphasizes. Information about reservations, costs, and stops can be found at the website for Airport Limousine:

➤ **webservice.limousinebus.co.jp/web/en/Top.aspx**

Arriving at Narita Airport
STEP BY STEP

If you arrive at Narita Airport, your step-by-step procedure for getting into Tokyo will be very similar to what it is from Haneda, with a few differing details. Narita is farther from Tokyo than Haneda is, and takes more time to travel from, but you still have at least three convenient options.

NARITA OPTION 1

Purchase a ticket for the Keisei Skyliner Express into Tokyo and combine it with a "Welcome! Tokyo Subway Ticket" pass.

At Narita, just as at Haneda, you can buy a great combo of a train ticket and subway pass that will get you into and around Tokyo.

Step One: At Narita Airport, go to a **Skyliner and Keisei Information Center or a Skyliner Ticket Counter**. These are located either in the Terminal 1 Station or in Terminals 2-3 Station. To find them, go down the escalator a level from where you leave immigration and customs.

Step Two: At the information center or counter, purchase what they call the "Keisei Skyliner & Tokyo Subway Ticket." This includes both a train ticket and the "Welcome! Tokyo Subway Ticket" pass that is good for 24, 48, or 72 hours (see previous chapter).

Step Three: With the ticket and pass in hand, use the train ticket to ride the Keisei Skyliner Express to Tokyo's Nippori or Ueno stations. (Ueno Station has more connections.)

Step Four: From there, use your Welcome! Tokyo Subway Ticket pass to take the subway wherever you need to go. *Remember that you must activate your subway pass with a gate agent the first time you use it.*

Note that this combo train ticket and subway pass can also be purchased at Narita's Terminal 1 Travel Center. For more details, check:

➤ **www.keisei.co.jp/keisei/tetudou/skyliner/us/findus/index.php**

or

➤ **www.keisei.co.jp/keisei/tetudou/skyliner/us/tickets/subway.php**

For an excellent tutorial on the above procedure, watch the ONE GOOD DREAM video:

➤ **www.youtube.com/watch?v=I4BrqGKsGvc**

Also note that if you choose not to use the subway system, Ueno and Nippori Stations offer excellent connections to various JR train lines, including the Yamanote Line. In other words, you can just buy a ticket for the Keisei Skyliner Express without the subway pass to get you into Tokyo. Once there, you can use your JR Pass or an IC card to ride whichever trains you wish.

NARITA OPTION 2

At Narita Airport, exchange your JR Pass voucher for your JR Pass and use it to obtain a ticket for the Narita Express, or "N'EX" train, into Tokyo.

Japan Railways (JR) offers their own express train from Narita into Tokyo. It is called the Narita Express, or N'EX:

➤ **www.jreast.co.jp/multi/en/nex/**

If you have a JR Pass voucher, simply exchange it for your actual JR Pass at a JR office at Narita Airport. When you do, ask for a ticket for the N'EX train and use that ticket to ride into Tokyo.

While slower than the Keisei Skyliner, the N'EX train stops at several major JR stations in Tokyo. One of these is likely to be close to your hotel, but if not, simply use your JR Pass to transfer to another JR line that will get you where you want to go.

Several things to note here:

- Although all of the N'EX trains stop at Tokyo Station and Shinagawa, from there they diverge into three different routes, so if you plan to go to Yokohama or Shinjuku, for example, make sure you are on the correct train–or transfer to the correct train once you reach Tokyo Station.
- You don't *need* to have a JR Pass to ride the N'EX train. Instead you can buy an individual one-way or round-trip ticket.[6]
- If you find that when you arrive at one of the Tokyo JR stations, you still need to use the subway to reach your hotel, you can

[6] See www.jreast.co.jp/multi/en/nex/tickets/

Most people exchange their JR Pass vouchers for their JR Passes immediately upon arrival at the airport, but if you don't need your pass right away, you can avoid long lines by waiting a day or two and visiting one of the numerous JR ticket offices in major stations.

pay for your ride(s) with an IC card or use a "Welcome! Tokyo" subway pass. If you failed to buy the "Welcome! Tokyo" subway pass at the airport and decide you want one after all, you can buy one at several train stations in Tokyo. A list of locations can be found at:

➤ **www.tokyometro.jp/tst/en/ticket-overseas-local.html**

NARITA OPTION 3

Ride local trains or buses.

If you don't want to buy any kind of (subway or JR) pass, a third option is to buy a Suica or Pasmo IC card at Narita Airport, charge it up with a few thousand yen, and ride local JR or Keisei trains into the city. The Keisei Narita Sky Access train, for instance, will take you into Ueno station, and is cheaper than the faster Skyliner train that runs along the same line. You can also ride the JR Narita Line to Chiba Station, where you will transfer to the Sobu Rapid Line to take you into Tokyo Station. Some slower JR trains also run directly from Narita into Tokyo, though not quite as frequently. Bus options are also available. These other options can save you money, but might end up being slower and more complicated than if you stick with Options 1 & 2 above. You can find out more information on these other options by doing an internet search such as "Getting from Narita Airport into Tokyo"–or asking the information desk at Narita once you arrive.

Again, this may all sound a bit scary, but you'll be surprised how smoothly it will go. To help ease your anxiety, Tokyo Metro has a great page that neatly diagrams the options above at:

➤ **www.tokyometro.jp/en/tips/from_airport/index.html**

I also recommend spending some time studying a Tokyo subway map, such as the one found here:

➤ **www.tokyometro.jp/en/subwaymap/**

and perusing the Tokyo JR map that can be found here:

➤ **www.jrailpass.com/pdf/maps/JRP_tokyo_metropolitan_map.pdf**

To help even more, let's take closer looks at using the **Japan Railways** (JR) system, various subway systems, and other transportation options for both local and long-distance travel.

WELCOME SUICA AND PASMO PASSPORT CARDS

The Japanese have come up with special IC cards for foreign visitors called the "Welcome Suica" and "Pasmo Passport" cards. The major differences between these and regular Suica and Pasmo cards appear to be that the former do not require a 500-yen deposit to buy the card and have different, colorful designs on them. These tourist cards, however, are also good for only 28 days from the time of purchase, so overall they seem a bit of much ado about nothing. My daughter and I went ahead and bought regular Suica cards and didn't worry about the 500-yen deposit because with the cute little penguin on them, they made nice mementos to take back home. Besides, if we decide to head back to Japan tomorrow, the cards will still be valid for immediate use!

Timely Note: At the time of this writing, sales of regular Suica and Pasmo cards had been suspended because of the global semiconductor shortage. You can still load the cards onto a phone, and Welcome Suica and Pasmo Passport cards are still on sale at limited locations. Before your trip, be sure to get the latest updates by checking:

➤ **www.jreast.co.jp/e/pass/suica.html**

and

➤ **www.pasmo.co.jp/visitors/en/normalpasmo/**

Using Japan Railways (JR) Trains

Now that you know what to do as soon as you arrive in Tokyo, let's start to complete your understanding of train travel by talking more about Japan's most important train operator, Japan Railways. As I mentioned before, Japan's national rail company runs both local and long-distance trains throughout the country, and your JR Pass will work on each. In Tokyo, Kyoto, Osaka, and many other large cities, in fact, you often have a choice between taking a JR train or a local subway line to get around town. If your JR Pass is already activated and you don't have a subway pass, choosing the JR alternatives will save you money. Before we discuss the long-distance JR trains, though, a brief look at the local lines will be helpful.

Astonishingly, JR's Yamanote Line carries more than four million people per day—and is a popular choice for travelers visiting Tokyo.

LOCAL TRAVEL

In Tokyo, the busiest, and often the most useful JR local line is the **Yamanote Line.** This runs in a giant loop, both clockwise and counter-clockwise, through almost every important station hub in the city center. In fact, many people plan their Tokyo stays so that they *only* have to use this line. This is fine if you are patient, but to go from one side of town to the other, you'll have to proceed in a long, slow arc that can waste a lot of time. Often, a better alternative is to cut across town using the **JR Chuo Line.** The Chuo Line also runs west to Studio Ghibli if you are lucky enough to score tickets.

If Tokyo Disney is on your itinerary, the **JR Keiyo Line** from Tokyo Station is your best bet. This line also stops at Kasai-Rinkai Park, a great place to go birding or just get a shot of nature. Other local JR lines will take you in all directions including the mountain areas of Hakone, the city of Yokohama, and the seaside town of Kamakura.

Major cities besides Tokyo also have useful local JR lines. In Kyoto, we rode the **Sagano Line** out to Arashiyama to go birding and visit the famous bamboo grove there. The **JR Nara Line** will take you to the Fushimi Inari Taisha shrine complex and then continues to the popular temple town of Nara. Meanwhile, the **JR Kyoto Line** goes to Osaka–which also has its own JR local lines including the **Osaka Loop (Kanjo) Line** circling the city. A complete Kyoto transit map can be found at:

➤ **www.jrpass.com/maps/map_kyoto_metro.pdf**

while an Osaka map can be found at:

➤ **subway.osakametro.co.jp/en/guide/routemap.php**

Note that to board almost any of these trains using your JR Pass, all you have to do is run your pass through the magnetic slot in a gate, walk through when it opens, (retrieving your pass as you do), find your train, and board.

INTERCITY TRAVEL—SHINKANSEN

As useful as JR's local trains are, most first-timers to Japan will be itching to ride JR's intercity trains–especially the shinkansen, or bullet trains. These trains truly are a joy to experience. My daughter and I first rode high-speed trains in Taiwan, and couldn't wait to ride them in Japan. Our first opportunity came when rain in Tokyo convinced us

The shinkansen, are without question the rock stars of Japan's rail network, transporting travelers at up to 200 miles per hour.

to take a spur-of-the-moment day trip north to Sendai. The ride met all of our expectations, not only for its comfort and smoothness, but for the remarkable scenery we passed through. It gave us our first feel for the immensity of Tokyo, but also took us through lovely rural countryside.

While you can just run your JR Pass through a ticket gate to use JR's local trains, you will want to use your JR Pass to reserve seats and obtain tickets for shinkansen. Strictly speaking, you do not need a reservation for all of the shinkansen as some of them have "non-reserved" cars in which you can take your chances on getting a seat—or stand, if no seat is available. However, trains can and do fill up, and especially if you want to sit together with your traveling companions, reservations are highly recommended. For popular routes, or during busy times of the year, this should be done several days in advance, but for many routes during normal seasons you can probably reserve and obtain your tickets immediately before you get on the train. We

While you may wish to reserve your first train tickets at a JR office, don't be surprised if you find yourself quickly graduating to self-serve ticket machines. Note the button at the bottom of the screen especially for Japan Rail Pass holders.

at first reserved tickets at JR offices in train stations, but as our confidence grew, we "graduated" to using the self-serve machines. These machines are easy to use and come in especially handy when the JR offices have long lines. For a good tutorial on using them, check out the ONE GOOD DREAM video at:

➤ **www.youtube.com/watch?v=DjltyiVnr_w**

To get the most out of your JR Pass, you'll probably be tempted to ride as many shinkansen as possible. On first trips, most people end up riding them on the Tokyo-Kyoto-Osaka-Hiroshima corridor, but this amazing high-speed network runs pretty much the length and breadth of the country. My daughter and I discovered, though, that the regular JR intercity trains offer plenty of charms of their own.

INTERCITY TRAVEL—TRADITIONAL TRAINS

While shinkansen ply the major routes between urban centers, JR runs plenty of traditional, aka "slower," trains to get you where you are going. Slower, though, does not necessarily mean worse. JR's traditional trains actually move along at a good clip, and go to a much greater variety of places than the super-speedy shinkansen. They can also help you soak in the scenery a lot better.

My favorite train ride of our entire trip probably was the "Thunderbird" from Kyoto north to the coastal town of Kanazawa. This train cruised along the startlingly large Lake Biwa before entering into a gorgeous mountainous region, only to descend back on to an impressive flat plain that continued to Kanazawa. Had we been on a bullet train, we wouldn't have had the time to appreciate this gorgeous journey, but the train we rode proved just right. On the trip, we saw recently-built portions of a new shinkansen that will connect Kyoto and Kanazawa directly, but I hope they keep the old line for those who want to savor the journey.

Note that for these longer, slower rides, you will want to reserve seats and obtain tickets in advance just as you do for the shinkansen.

DIFFERENT JR REGIONS

To wrap up this chapter, a reminder that Japan Railways is divided into different regions, and you *can* buy a JR pass that covers only a particular region. If you look up various prices, though, you'll find that you don't end up saving that much. Worse, you risk getting stuck with extra costs if you spontaneously decide to travel outside of that region. Because of this, I again recommend just getting the overall, country-wide JR Pass if you plan to do any kind of serious travel.

An exception for some is to buy JR passes that cover only the Tokyo or greater Kyoto-Osaka regions. You can purchase these for one or several days and they are very reasonably priced. For more information, see

JR Tokyo Wide Pass:

➤ **www.jreast.co.jp/multi/en/pass/tokyowidepass.html**

JR Kansai Area Pass (Kyoto-Osaka region):

➤ **www.westjr.co.jp/global/en/ticket/pass/kansai/**

More information and ideas on passes also can be found on the very useful travel website of **Tokyo Cheapo** (tokyocheapo.com).

Final Note: Whichever JR pass you decide to buy, don't lose it! JR will not replace lost passes. Tessa and I had a close call when she dropped her pass while we were riding a Tokyo subway train. As we were rumbling along, I felt a tug on my pant leg, and looked down to see an elderly woman pointing to the floor. There was my daughter's JR Pass! Without that woman's kindness, we would have been out several hundred dollars. If you *do* lose your pass and have an idea where you lost it, check the lost and found at the nearest JR office. Since only you can use your pass, and since the Japanese are extremely honest, there's a chance someone will turn it in.

友 *ROY RECOMMENDS*

Night, or Sleeper, Trains

Once upon a time, many popular overnight trains with sleeper cars criss-crossed Japan. Alas, with the advent of the shinkansen, most of these overnight trains have disappeared. The sole survivor is the Sunrise Express running between Tokyo and either Izumo or Takamatsu. A JR Pass will cover the basic ticket, but you will have to pay an additional fare for various private compartments. These tickets also sell out quickly. To learn more, read:

- **www.jrailpass.com/blog/night-trains-sunrise-express**

and

- **www.japan-guide.com/e/e2356.html**

Using Japan's Subways and Independent Operators

We've already discussed a fair amount about Japan subways—and by "subway" I also loosely refer to elevated trains, trams, funiculars, monorails, and any other local "non-JR" transport systems—but it's worth going into a bit more detail now. Major systems such as Tokyo's subway system are generally publicly owned, but dozens of privately-owned railways also ply various routes, and you undoubtedly will find yourself on a couple of these private lines. The Keikyu train from Haneda Airport and Keisei Skyliner from Narita are prominent examples of trains run by private corporations. In Kamakura, my daughter and I rode what has got to be the cutest little train anywhere, the Enoshima Electric Railway—another independent line.

But let's start with the mother of all subway systems—the Tokyo subway.

As stated earlier, one look at the Tokyo subway map is enough to make a would-be traveler swear off of Japan forever. However, I'm here to tell you that despite the labyrinthine confusion of color-coded routes and stations, the system is surprisingly easy to navigate. Even using a printed map, it's fairly simple to see which lines to ride from Point A to Point B, including where to transfer from one line to another. Anyone who has ever ridden the New York subway or London Underground will quickly grasp what to do—and if you don't, Google Maps will do it for you. Simply type in your current location and your intended destination, and Maps will plot every subway move you'll need to make.

One thing that isn't obvious are the two little symbols you'll see at various subway stations. At first I thought they referred to specific subway lines, such as the Tozai or Asakusa lines. Instead, they indicate which of two public corporations manages a particular line. A stylized white "M" on a blue background means that a line is run by Tokyo Metro. A stylized green ginkgo leaf (also the symbol for metropolitan Tokyo itself) means that a line is run by the Toei Corporation. In other words, a visitor can ignore these symbols and focus on the name of the actual line you are trying to take.

At first glance, Tokyo's subway system can feel pretty intimidating. However, great signage and frequent trains make the system both easy and enjoyable to use.

The Welcome! Tokyo Subway Ticket pass provides a low-cost, convenient way for visitors to ride any of Tokyo's 13 different subway lines and, as indicated earlier, you can buy 24-, 48-, or 72-hour versions of the pass. If 72 hours isn't long enough, hey, just go buy another one!

Here are some other tips for using Tokyo's subways:

- Whenever possible, plot your subway route before you leave your hotel room or other location. This helps increase your awareness of what you are doing, and helps you spot subway stations and other landmarks you'll need to navigate your trip.
- During rush hours, many subways can be packed. If you can leave a bit earlier or later, your ride will be more pleasant.
- Engage your full etiquette tools when riding a subway. We Americans and many other foreigners are basically uncouth barbarians compared to the Japanese, so while riding keep your voice down, don't eat and drink, never litter, give up your seat to the elderly and others who need it, and keep your kids under control–even if that means using a shock collar. Oh yes, and **wear a mask to protect other passengers**!
- Keep your pass or ticket in a secure location that is easily accessible. For instance, I kept mine in a small, zipped pocket of the cargo pants I wore.
- If you're only occasionally going to be riding the subway, you can use your IC card to pay for individual rides instead of buying a pass. As explained earlier, you can recharge these cards at various machines and at convenience stores, too. IC cards can also be used for local buses and almost all other transit systems, such as our cute little train in Kamakura. If you're hungry or thirsty, you can even use your IC card to pay for a snack at the nearest convenience store!

Although this chapter focuses on Tokyo, everything in it applies to Japan's other subway systems, too. Kyoto and many other large cities have excellent subway lines and they all basically work in the same way.

As I discussed earlier, you will want to find places to stay that are close to at least one, and preferably two or three, different subway

IC cards are the best way to pay for rides on Japan's many independent transport systems, such as the ultra-adorable Enoshima Electric Railway.

stations. I chose our first Tokyo hotel partly because it sat within a five-minute walk of two different subway stations and Tokyo Station itself. In Kyoto, our hotel sat about eight minutes' walk from two different stations. We were especially grateful for this since we ended up walking between six and ten miles a day every day we were in Japan. Not having to make an additional long trudge between a subway station and our hotel proved a great relief to our tired feet.

Buses, Taxis, and Ubers

You can probably tell that I have an obvious bias toward rail-based transportation over buses and taxis. That's partly because, like private cars, buses and taxis have to deal with street traffic, a potentially frustrating experience. I also find that buses are often less comfortable than trains while taxis contribute to an inordinate share of pollution and congestion, neither of which sits high on my "favorite things" list. The main reason I prefer trains, though, is that I know exactly where to find them and exactly where they are going.

That said, during our Japan trip I had positive experiences with both buses and taxis. Most Tokyo buses are run by Toei—the same public outfit that runs several of Tokyo's subway lines, and has the

Thanks to Japan's less congested streets, buses are almost as easy to use as subways. Google Maps is a huge help in locating bus stops and timetables.

green ginkgo leaf as its symbol. Some buses accept cash, but it's a lot easier to buy a day pass from the bus driver and use it all day, or tap your IC card on the little pad at the bus's front door (another great reason to buy an IC card). The buses charge a flat rate per ride, and if you are going to take more than two bus rides in a day, the day pass is a good idea.

I found Japanese city buses to be clean and efficient, if not quite as on-time as the subways. Like the subways, they have video screens that alert you (both in Japanese and English) to the next several stops. Finding a bus stop can be tricky, but once again, Google Maps comes to the rescue. After you enter your destination, Maps tells you where to find stops for the "bus parts" of your route—and with remarkable accuracy.

More information about Tokyo's buses can be found at:

➤ **www.kotsu.metro.tokyo.jp/eng/services/bus.html**

Special note: Japan Railways runs their own local buses (marked with the "JR" logo) in many cities, and you can use your JR Pass to ride these at no extra cost. For more information, check out:

➤ **www.jrailpass.com/buses#buses-covered-by-the-japan-rail-pass**

A final note on buses is that Tokyo used to have a reputation for heavy traffic congestion—and is sometimes still presented that way—but during our visit I found the central areas remarkably uncongested compared to American cities. I kept looking for traffic jams, especially at rush hour, and finally found one—sort of, at about 5 p.m. on a freeway in Shibuya—but even then, traffic was moving along at a clip that would have made L.A. commuters brown with envy. I mention this because Japan's buses seem to move fairly quickly, making it efficient to use one. The same applies to our next subject: taxis.

友 *ROY RECOMMENDS*

SLEEPER BUSES

As much as I love trains, Roy suggests keeping an open mind about long-distance buses, also called highway or sleeper buses. "The sleeper bus is getting bigger and bigger in Japan," Roy explains, "especially among young people and budget travelers. Some buses are so luxurious that you can call them first-class buses. The night bus is absolutely a game changer. You can not only reduce your transportation cost and time, but also save the accommodation fee for the night. In every big city, there are some shower room services close to major stations, and these are open 24/7. The showers before and after the long bus ride absolutely improve your sleep quality and make you refreshed to start a new day in a new place."

To learn more about the highway buses plying the route between the Tokyo and Osaka regions, check out the following websites:

➤ **www.japan.travel/en/plan/getting-around/buses/**

➤ **www.kanto-bus.co.jp/english/nightway/dream-sleeper/**

➤ **www.willerexpress.com/en/bus/seat/reborn/**

TAXIS

We hadn't planned on taking any taxis in Japan, but did end up doing so. It's quite feasible to flag one down on the street, but for my trips, I asked our hotel receptionists to call them. Easy peasy. You can also find taxi-hailing apps, similar to the Uber app, for your phone with a quick web search.

Our first taxi ride took us up a hefty hill to the spectacular Kiyomizu-dera Temple—truly a must-see place for anyone visiting Kyoto. It was a warm afternoon and we'd already walked about six miles that day, so not having to slog up the hill proved well worth the ten dollars or so I shelled out.

I hired my second taxi to take me out to a birding area in Kanazawa, about half an hour from our hotel. I could have ridden a bus, but it would have taken twice as long, and I wasn't sure where it would drop me off. Like our first taxi driver, this one spoke very little English to go with my very poor Japanese, but using Google Maps on my phone, I was easily able to convey where I wanted to go.

Choosing a taxi in this case turned out to be a very good move, because the park where I ended up was at least a mile or two from any main bus routes. Even better, once we got there, my driver offered to come back and get me in a couple of hours, saving me a lot of sweat and stress. I had expected to pay about $50 each way for these rides, but it ended up costing only about half of that—in part because **there is no tipping in Japan**!

Roy also points out that especially when you are traveling in a larger group, taxis often end up being your cheapest, most efficient option for getting somewhere. To wrap up, do use the trains as much as you can, but keep in mind that in Japan both buses and taxis are excellent, affordable options when you need them.

UBER AND LYFT

You may be asking "What about Uber and Lyft?" At the time of this writing, Lyft does not appear to operate in Japan, while Uber's coverage is much more limited than it is here in the U.S. and many other areas. Furthermore, Japan's taxi services are so clean, pleasant, and reasonably-priced that most people tend to use Uber in only specific situations, such as getting rides to airports. I'm guessing that this situation will continue to evolve, however, so if you are an Uber-holic, be sure to check for the latest news by doing some web searches online.

Chances are that transportation in Japan will not make you as frustrated as this guy!

Pocket wifi devices and SIM cards are widely available in Japan, and can be reserved ahead of time for pick-up at the airport upon your arrival.

PART IV
Connections and Cash
楽

Phones and Wifi

In our modern world, making sure that your smartphone operates seamlessly while traveling Japan is going to rate as one of your top priorities. To ensure you stay fully connected, you basically have three choices:

- Sign up for a temporary international travel plan from your current cellular provider.
- Buy a SIM card for your phone that allows you to access the internet, and possibly make calls, in Japan.
- Use only wifi while in Japan and communicate through programs such as WhatsApp, Skype, or FaceTime.

Option 1: Use Your Current Provider

The first option, using your current provider, is probably the easiest and most convenient choice–but not necessarily the cheapest. At the time of this writing, our own carrier (Verizon) offers plans that will either charge you $10/day or $130 for a 30-day trip for each phone, and for our three-week trip to Japan, I opted for the latter plan. Yeah, it's a lot, but for us, not having to worry about getting connected when we got there was well worth it. Also, our iPhones were "carrier locked" to Verizon so that we could not swap out SIM cards even if we wanted to.

A quick look at other large cellular companies show that they offer similar international plans–some of them a bit cheaper. With these plans, you have to sign up ahead of time by getting on the company website, but at least with Verizon I've found that the plans have worked flawlessly both in Japan and in other countries I've traveled.

Option 2: Buy a SIM Card for Japan

Many phones allow you to swap out your SIM card for one that provides services in a new place. A SIM card is a tiny electronic card or chip that allows you to connect to a cellular network. The one in your phone allows you to connect to your current provider's network, but when you travel to another country you can buy a pre-paid SIM that allows you to connect to a cellular network in that country.

The main advantage of buying a SIM for the country you're traveling in is that it can save you money. A Japan SIM, though, does come with some disadvantages:

- If you have a "locked" phone like I do, you can't use another SIM card anyway.
- You will have to reconfigure your phone to the new SIM and may encounter compatibility problems.
- Most SIMs in Japan are data-only, and won't have a phone number connected with them. You can text and search the web, and make calls using a program such as WhatsApp—but you won't be able to just call someone like you usually do. One exception at the time of this writing is that **Mobal Japan Unlimited** (Mobal.com) does offer SIMs with both data and calling.
- **Perhaps most important**, SIM plans may not save you that much over just getting an international plan from your current provider—at least not enough to justify the hassle.

If you are comfortable swapping SIMs and want to go that route, you can pre-order one and pick it up at the airport upon your arrival—or in some cases have it delivered to your hotel. You can also get one from an automated machine at the airport or elsewhere. For more information, the **Tokyo Cheapo** website has some great articles on the pros and cons of international phone plans versus SIM cards, and which SIM cards to use if you go the latter route. You also can find information about SIMs at a site such as **Sakura Mobile** (sakuramobile.jp), a large provider that has a whole section on travel SIMs and wifi.

Be aware that newer phones build SIM cards right into the phone hardware so that they cannot be swapped out. Instead, you can buy an "eSIM"—basically a software version of a swappable SIM card that you download onto your phone. Just as with physical SIMs, the eSIMs of some phones may be locked to a particular carrier, but most phones will allow you to buy and download eSIMs, and some travelers swear by them. To learn more, several good articles on SIMs and eSIMS are available with a quick web search.

Option 3: Use Wifi Only

Travelers who really want to save money, and don't need to make regular phone calls, can dispense with both SIMs and international calling plans, and instead rely solely on wifi while traveling Japan. With wifi access only, you can still make phone calls through WhatsApp,

Skype, or FaceTime—but, again, won't be able to just call anyone using your phone as you do at home.

The one problem with wifi in Japan is that the country doesn't have the coverage that you'll find in the U.S. and other countries. Of the six different hotels we stayed at in Japan, for instance, only one had decent wifi. The good news? This can be overcome by renting a **pocket wifi** device.

A pocket wifi is basically a little rechargeable electronic router that you carry around with you. It can be connected to several devices at once and is very affordable at about five or six bucks a day at the time of this writing.

Many companies offer portable wifi devices for rent. When you order your JR Pass voucher, in fact, the site gives you the option of also renting a portable wifi router from **Ninja WiFi**, a company that comes highly recommended. As soon as you arrive in Japan, you simply go to the company's booth at the airport and they get you set up. You can return the device at the airport as you leave—or drop it off at another specified location.

Money

One cool thing about Japan is that cold hard cash remains a vital part of the economy. As mentioned earlier, many merchants, including a fair number of restaurants, only take cash, so it's a good idea to always carry twenty or thirty thousand yen (a couple of hundred bucks) around with you.

But let's start at the beginning. To travel in Japan, you will need the following financial tools:

- Credit cards—preferably at least both a Visa and American Express card.
- An ATM card that allows you to withdraw cash in the form of yen from your home savings and checking accounts.
- U.S. dollars (or your own country's currency) for emergencies.

CREDIT CARDS

Despite the widespread use of cash in Japan, most places do take credit cards—especially Visa and American Express. Supposedly, more merchants accept Visa cards, but I did not find that to be an issue. Other major cards in use include Mastercard, Discover Card, Diner's Club, and Japan's own JCB card.

Because I earn airline miles on it, I used my airline AmEx card for the vast majority of our major purchases in Japan including paying for our hotels, daily visits to convenience stores **(see "Convenience Stores" in Part VI)**, entry to Tokyo Disney and other tourist sites, restaurants, train station kiosks, and gift stores. My card gave me the latest exchange rate without charging me a foreign transaction fee, but **check your card terms, because many credit cards do charge additional foreign transaction fees when you use them abroad.**

It's also an excellent idea to let your credit card company know that you will be traveling before you go. Some companies, if they suddenly see a charge from Tokyo, will automatically lock your card so that you'll be unable to use it. I had to call one of my companies to let them know I'd be traveling, but was able to notify another by logging into my account online.

One last suggestion for credit cards is to **keep at least one of them in a separate place.** If you lose your purse or wallet containing *all* of your cash and credit cards, well, the next few days are going to be rough. When I travel, I always leave one card in my wallet or money belt, and keep another back in the hotel room safe or zipped in a secure pocket.

ATM CARDS

An ATM or debit card is another essential financial tool for traveling Japan. An ATM or debit card, of course, allows you to withdraw cash from thousands of Automated Teller Machines, or ATMs, and in most Japanese cities, ATMs are as common as pigeons. Not all of them accept foreign bank cards, but most of them do, including ATMs at convenience stores, post offices, hotels, tourist sites, restaurants, and many other places. If you run into a machine that doesn't take your card, you will generally find one that does within a block or two—but check with your bank *before* you leave your home country to see what kind of coverage you will have.

Generally, there is a maximum limit you can withdraw from an ATM at a time, and a maximum limit per day, but in Japan these are fairly high (about 50,000 and 200,000 yen respectively) and shouldn't pose a problem. You will also likely get a better exchange rate using an ATM than you will by going to a traditional currency exchange place at an airport or tourist area.

Remember that most bank cards charge transaction fees at ATMs outside of their own networks, so withdrawing a larger amount from an ATM in each transaction will generally save you money. Before you go, you might also want to inquire about bank cards that don't charge fees abroad.

If you know your pin number, you can use your credit card to withdraw cash from an ATM, **but most companies will start charging you interest on this cash advance immediately instead of letting you pay it off interest-free with your next credit card statement.** In other words, it will be cheaper to use your bank card to get cash. And speaking of . . .

CASH

We've already covered how to get local currency from an ATM in Japan, but let's talk a little more about cash. As discussed earlier, many Japanese merchants prefer cash or only accept cash. This means you are always going to want plenty of "walking around" money on you. Fortunately, Japan is one of the world's safest countries, so carrying around thirty or forty thousand yen is not going to make you a target for pickpockets or purse-snatchers.

The main risk to carrying more cash is that you might accidentally lose it, so figure out a system to prevent that. I usually wear cargo pants that come with an abundance of deep and/or zippable pockets. This allows me to feel pretty secure about carrying around my cash, credit cards, passport, and other essentials. I carry all of these in a **money belt** that fits snugly down in a deep pocket—but in Japan, a money belt (whether you place it in a pocket or around your waist as intended) isn't necessary. You can just stick with a regular wallet as you would at home. Similarly, most hotel rooms are very safe, so another option is to go out with some cash, a credit card, your health insurance card, and your passport zipped into a pocket and leave your bulky purse or wallet back in the room safe.

One of your first concerns upon arriving in Japan is to acquire some Japanese yen, the national currency. Some people exchange dollars for yen *before* they leave their home country. **Don't do this.**

In Japan, many merchants still take cash only, so it's a good idea to carry a few thousand yen with you at all times.

Back home, your exchange rate will be terrible, and really, there is no need for it. As soon as you clear customs and immigration in Japan, you will see plenty of ATMs where you can obtain your first wad of Japanese cash.

Even after you arrive in Japan, avoid exchanging U.S. currency for yen at one of those exchange counters that abound at airports and tourist areas. You aren't likely to get a great rate from them—and you'll want to save your dollars or other currency for emergencies. If you do want to exchange paper dollars or other money for yen, automated "smart exchange" machines can do this for you. I haven't used one, but I hear the exchange rates are quite reasonable. These machines accept about a dozen different international currencies and are located in various airports, train stations, and other locations.

How much U.S. or other cash should you bring? That partly depends on how lavishly you spend. Personally, I ask myself, "Okay, how much will I need to survive for a few days if my credit cards suddenly stop working, or I encounter an emergency?" I figure it might take a few days to get a replacement credit card or other similar item, so I generally bring about a thousand bucks—enough to pay for a few nights' lodging, food, and so forth.

Although the Japanese like to have fun, they show great respect for personal space on the subway and in other public places.

PART V

Showing Respect

楽

Proper Behavior, Step by Step

Let's be honest. Americans in particular haven't earned a great reputation while traveling to other countries. Many Americans are loud, obnoxious, and totally impervious to how others are behaving around them. This seems to be especially true for those traveling on tours that rapidly whisk people from one place to another with almost no meaningful local interaction. I can't count how many times I've seen Americans "on tour" complaining about this or that, as if a host country should be bending over backwards to accommodate the economic imperialists gracious enough to visit them.

Fortunately, I've also seen plenty of American travelers trying hard to show respect and actually learn something about a culture while traveling, and if you are reading this, you probably fall into this second category.

That said, manners and behavior in Japan are complex, and my guess is that it might take years to understand everything that may or may not be considered rude or polite. Fortunately, our "inside man," Roy, is here to help with the essentials. The advice below comes mainly from my own observations and experiences in Japan, reading up on the culture, and common universal protocols I've discovered traveling other countries. Roy helps provide insight and meaning to these topics, so if you follow the steps below, well, we're confident you'll be covered!

Step One: Smile—But Keep Your Eyes to Yourself

Almost universally, a smile sends a positive message to another person, regardless if you share a common language or culture. An exchange of smiles, though, usually requires eye contact—and that's not something that will happen a lot in Japan. Even if you are curious about someone, the polite thing seems to be to keep your eyes to yourself, or at least not look at others too pointedly.

"Eye contact things are very complicated in Japan," Roy explains. "Usually we don't look at each other's faces in daily conversation. But when you are serious, eye contact is very important—like apologies, serious talks, and when a man has to explain to his wife about a girl he was walking with the other day! Basically," he sums up, "we are just shy, and eye contact makes us uncomfortable and awkward."

Nevertheless, if you do catch someone looking at you, be sure to smile back at them. This happened to us a number of times and initiated some very nice little exchanges. Of course, wearing face masks can make it more difficult to detect a smile (see below), but smiles can show up in a person's eyes, too, so be observant.

Step Two: Walk on the Left

It's a fact: Japanese walk, ride, and drive on the left. This sounds easy to adapt to, but we messed this up *so many times.* To make matters worse, sometimes people walk on the right for no apparent reason. If you are trying to walk down a busy sidewalk or through a subway station, the best course of action is to just follow the "main current" of foot traffic as far as you can. **Pay special attention when crossing streets.** Americans and (most) Europeans are used to looking to our left to see if traffic is coming, but in Japan, cars usually will be approaching from the *right.* "Once, my colleague driver hit a woman from a country where people drive their car on the right side of the roads," Roy recounts. "She checked only to her left and started to cross the street." **Bottom line: Make it a habit to look both ways *several times* before you step off a curb.**

Step Three: When in Doubt, Bow

Bowing serves several functions in Japan. It replaces a handshake as a way to greet someone. It serves as an apology–but also as a thank you. It doesn't need to be a full bow. A half- or one-quarter bow, or even a sincere nod of the head, will do. The main point is that it's almost never a mistake to bow, so when in doubt . . . bow!

Step Four: Talk Quietly–and Stay Off Your Phone

If you're paying attention, one thing you'll notice riding a Japanese train or subway is that you never hear people talking loudly–or at all, in most cases. This also applies to temples and shrines. When you *do* hear someone talking loudly in such a place, chances are it's an American or European. If you want to talk to your traveling companion(s), keep your voices way down–almost to a whisper–to avoid disturbing others. A corollary to this is **never talk on your cell phone while riding a bus, subway, or other form of public transportation.** This is disturbing to others–both in Japan and elsewhere, though some people remain stubbornly unaware of this.

Step Five: Take Your Shoes Off

When entering a house, shrine, and many public establishments, it's considered polite to take off your shoes. In fact, it's remarkable to me how this custom has caught on in many places around the world, so it shouldn't be too hard to remember when you're in Japan. That said, we had to remove our shoes only at a couple of shrines and one restaurant that I can recall. Before entering a place, glance around to see what everyone else is doing–and follow suit.

Step Six: Cover Up Your Tattoos

Tattoos in Japan are generally associated with the *yakuza*, or organized crime. In fact, many *onsen*, or public baths and hot springs, won't let you in with tattoos, so plan accordingly. Roy elaborates, "The influx of foreign tourists is changing Japanese society since many visitors have tattoos as fashion accessories. Many of us, including those in government, know these tattoos are just for fashion, and years ago the Japanese government released a guideline stating that the tourism industry should be tolerant to foreigners' tattoos. Some public/private swimming pools and onsens are adopting this guideline, but a majority of businesses are stubbornly following the old 'rules.' I recommend that all tattooed people check a facility's tattoo policy beforehand."

Step 7: Don't Stab or Pass Things with Your Chopsticks

Need I say more?

Step 8: Wear a Facemask in Public

Even before the pandemic, many Asians wore facemasks, and now the practice in Japan is almost universal. Many Americans and other visitors, however, seem to think this somehow infringes upon their right to . . . what, spread diseases? In any case, it's not about you. It's about protecting others around you, so if you don't want to wear a mask, well, consider visiting Las Vegas instead.

Step 9: Don't Tip!

This will undoubtedly be your favorite etiquette, ahem, tip, and it's true: Japanese do not accept gratuities–and, in fact, can be insulted by being offered one. Remembering this will save you face and money.

Roy recommends, though, that if someone does something nice for you to "tip" them with a sincere, personal thank you, or perhaps even a small gift. You might even want to pack a few little gift items in your suitcase before you leave your home country.

All of the above etiquette guidelines contribute to creating one of the most polite, respectful societies on the planet–a big reason people love going to Japan. On the other hand, the rules can make it very difficult to have a conversation with a Japanese resident. Still, it can happen. When Tessa and I were riding the cute little Enoshima Electric Railway in Kamakura, I noticed a young couple sitting across from us with a suitcase that had a big picture of Snoopy on it. I pointed to it and said, "Peanuts." At first, the couple seemed concerned that I needed something. Then, they realized what I was saying, and broke into smiles. There followed a fun, stilted conversation in my horrible Japanese and their slightly better English. Another woman next to us even jumped in and asked if she could translate for us. It turned into one of our most memorable and delightful experiences of the trip.

Navigating the Japanese Language

Whenever I mention traveling to Japan, the Number One question I receive is "What about the language?" For those of us brought up in the West, speaking Japanese, let alone reading and writing it, seems like an almost impossible task. Let me assure you–it is! At least for me. I spent a solid four months studying common words and phrases before going to Japan and the results were mediocre at best.

The good news is that Japan has made significant efforts to install English signage in most of the places you're likely to go. We found it a rare event when we couldn't find an English street sign or English translations of menu items. Trains, subways, and buses have generous English signage so you can tell where you are and which stops are coming up. It *does* happen that you run into a "No English Zone," but hey, that's part of the fun of travel. Would it really feel like an adventure if it were all just like being back home?

If you need more convincing, many Japanese also speak at least a little English. Most seem shy about it in the same way I would be hesitant to resurrect my junior high school French to a native speaker, but when push comes to shove, the basic words are in there. Once

Never fear, Japan has made significant efforts to install English signage—but it will still greatly enhance your experience to learn some basic Japanese words and phrases.

Japanese people warm up to their English, I found that most of them can communicate basics quite well. Other communication tools at your disposal include:

- Pointing things out on maps.
- Having hotel clerks write down destinations in Japanese so you can show the words to taxi drivers or a stranger when asking directions.
- Loudly crying for help.

Okay, maybe skip that last one. The bottom line is that you shouldn't let the difficulty of the Japanese language in any way dissuade you from visiting this remarkable country.

With that pep talk out of the way, my personal philosophy is that it's *always* good—not to mention respectful—to learn at least a few basic words and phrases when you plan to be a guest in a foreign country. As I indicated, acquiring even a little Japanese takes some diligence, but I found that I used almost all of the phrases I learned over and over again, greatly enriching my experience of being there.

The most useful phrases were different kinds of greetings, followed by asking what something is, how much it costs, and where a place is located. For these later questions I, of course, didn't understand the answers people gave me—but I did understand someone showing me numbers on a calculator or pointing in a particular direction. So learning a few phrases along with some basic numbers definitely paid off.

"What about Google Translate?" you may ask. GT truly is a remarkable tool, and I especially enjoy its camera feature, with which you can take photos of Japanese words and get them instantly translated. In general, though, I guess I'm just an old fart and prefer seeing what I can do with my own inferior brain.

So without further ado, below are the words and phrases I found most useful plus those that Roy felt would be most helpful. To the right are Roy's phonetic pronunciations of the Japanese equivalents. You'll see these pronunciations written in different ways and it will take your ear a bit of time to adjust to what the words really sound like once you get over there and start hearing them. For instance, "Good morning," in Japanese is written out "Ohayoh gozai masu," but I almost never actually heard the "-su" on the end of the phrase. Instead, the whole phrase sounded like "Ohio gozai-ee-mas." To help you out learning these, I recommend that you punch up Google Translate, type in the English word, wait for the Japanese translation, and then click the little speaker icon to hear how it is pronounced.

Also keep in mind that when asking a question, you can usually substitute the English name if you don't know the Japanese equivalent. For example, to ask where a toilet is, you could ask "Toilet doko desukah?" and people will understand you and point you in the right direction.

GREETINGS

Kon nichi wa.	Hello.
Ohayoh gozai masu.	Good morning.
Kon ban wah.	Good evening.
Hajimeh mashiteh.	Nice to meet you.
Sayoh nara.	Goodbye.
Mataneh.	See you later.

COURTESIES

Oneh gai shimasu.	Please.
Arigatou gozaimasu.	Thank you.
Doh itashi mashite.	You are welcome.
Suimasen.	Excuse me.
Gomen nasai.	I'm sorry.
Ohgenki desu kah?	How are you?
Genki des.	I am well.

BASIC EVERYDAY WORDS

Hai.	Yes.
I i ee.	No.
Dameh desu.	Don't do that.
Chotto mattee kudasai.	Hold on please.
Kekkoh desu.	No thank you.
...o kudasai.	I would like...please.
Nanjii?	What time?

FOOD AND DINING

Ohmizu o kudasai.	Water please.
Itadakimasu.	Let's eat.
Oishii.	Delicious.
Koreh wa nan desukah?	What is this?
...wa tabeh raree masen.	I can't eat. . .
Koreh wa ikura desukah?	How much does this cost?
Gochisoh sama deshita.	Thank you for the meal.

COMMUNICATING

Eigo deh oneh gai shimasu.	(Speak) English please.
Nihongo wa hanaseh masen.	I don't speak Japanese.
Eigo wa hanaseh masukah?	Do you speak English?
Wakarimasen.	I don't understand.
Mou ichidoh onegaishimasu.	Please repeat it again.
Yukkuri hanashiteh kudasai.	Can you please speak slowly?
Namaeh oh oshii eteh kudasai.	What is your name?
Watashino namaeh wa...	My name is...

DIRECTIONS

...wa doko desukah?	Where is ...?
Tasuketeh kudasai.	Can you please help me?
Koko ni ikitai desu.	I want to go here.
Doko.	Where.

Koko.	Here.
Koko wa doko desukah?	Where is here?
Ah soko.	There.
Deh guchi.	The exit.
Iiri guchi.	The entrance.
Toh i re.	The bathroom.

OTHER COMMON WORDS

Kawa	River
Mizu	Water
Koh en	Park
Dou ro (or Dori)	Road
Eeh ki	Station
Kei sa tsu	Police
Kon bee nii	Convenience store
Byoh inn	Hospital
Oh mii seh	Store/Shop
Nihon	Japan (the country)
Nihongo	Japanese (the language)
Toweereh	Toilet (or simply use the word "toilet")

NUMBERS

Ichi – 1 Nii – 2 Sann – 3 Shee/Yonn – 4 Goh – 5
Roku – 6 Nana/Shech – 7 Hachi – 8 Kyuu – 9 Jyuu – 10

Beyond the above words, many Japanese place names are derived from common words, and if you learn a few of them, it will help you appreciate and understand some of the names that you are seeing and hearing. Besides kawa, mizu, ko hen, and dori listed above, here are a few more you are likely to see on maps and signs:

Shima	Island
Hama	Beach, Shore
Hara, or Bara	Meadow, Prairie, Field
Yama	Mountain
Ki	Tree
Shin	New
Mono	Thing, Object
Hashi, or Bashi	Bridge
Machi	City, Town, Area
Oh	Big
Ko	Small
Ichi	One, First, Bes
Higashi	East
Minami	South
Nishi	West
Kita	North

Noodle places abound in Japan, offering delicious inexpensive meals almost any time of day.

PART VI

Food, or Eating till You Drop

楽

Food, The Big Picture

Ah, fooooooood.

While a potential visitor's top worry about Japan is the language, the top source of excitement tends to be its food. How could it be otherwise? Over the centuries, Japan has produced one of the world's great cuisines. Sushi, tempura, ramen, okonomiyaki, yakitori, udon noodles, soba noodles, dumplings, onigiri . . . well, the list is extensive and almost all of it is delicious. Learning about and trying Japan's incredible cuisine is the work of a lifetime and mostly beyond the scope of this guide. Fortunately, gazillions of Japan food-related guidebooks, blogs, television shows, podcasts, and YouTube videos lie at your fingertips, and if food is your main jam, you'll find no shortage of resources to learn more.

That doesn't mean we don't have plenty to discuss, so let's get started, step by step, beginning with how to find it.

If you're worried about where to find food in Japan, you'll laugh once you land there. Why? Because in Japan, food is *everywhere*. I don't think I've ever been to a country where food is more available—and not just the low-grade industrial food that Americans are used to. In Japan, even the "cheap stuff" is safe to eat and, more often than not, extraordinarily tasty.

The best way to begin is this: whenever you are hungry, grab the first interesting food item that you see and eat it. Each region of Japan has its own specialties, and the more you try, the more you'll discover what your favorites are. "But what if I don't like something?" you might ask.

My answer: "That's great!" Because if you find something you don't like, you will have had a valuable cultural experience that you can reminisce about later. Even better you can, ahem, *prawn off* your unwanted food on your travel partner and try something else that you'll probably like better. The important thing is to sample as much as you possibly can. In the process, you will create some of your best Japan memories, and discover genuine, mouth-watering treasures that you will return to again and again.

With that quick introduction, let's look at how to navigate some of your most important types of food hotspots.

SIT-DOWN RESTAURANTS AND CAFÉS

Not surprisingly, Japan has a lot of great restaurants, and if you are a real foodie, you'll want to do research ahead of time to learn the best ones wherever you are staying. Some of these will probably require reservations, so plan accordingly. Hotel desks often have lists of nearby recommended restaurants and these can come in handy. We especially relied on our hotel's list in Kyoto, where we ate at a great little okonomiyaki place and a truly wonderful–don't laugh–pizza place.

Part of the fun of traveling, though, is to try places you just happen to encounter. One evening after visiting the fabulous Kiyomizu-dera Temple in Kyoto, we decided to walk the long way back to our hotel through the old geisha district of Gion. We were both having blood sugar crashes and found ourselves on Hanamikoji Street, a long picturesque street lined with izakayas–small bar/restaurants with hanging red lanterns out front (see "**Roy Recommends: Omakase, Izakaya, Kaiseki**" on page 95). We couldn't tell what most of these places actually served, but we found one with a menu posted next to the door and decided to go for it. It turned out to be one of our favorite meals of the trip. Like many restaurants in Japan, the place could seat only perhaps twenty people at a time, giving it a relaxing, intimate atmosphere. Just to be conversational, I practiced my terrible Japanese with the waiter and he relayed my comments to the cooks behind the counter. They laughed appreciatively–whether at my comments or my poor Japanese, I'll never know. We decided to order teishokus, or "set meals,"[7] from the menu and every course turned out to be excellent.

We repeated this kind of experience several times in Japan, almost always with satisfying results, but to help alleviate any anxiety about this, let's look into some details.

Menus & Ordering

While many Japanese restaurants have menus in English, many do not. Usually, however, the menu has pictures of at least some of the food that is available, and by pointing to that picture, perhaps along

[7] A teishoku, or set meal, is one that comes with a number of pre-chosen items such as rice, miso soup, several little kinds of salads, and a main dish.

with some hand gestures or charades between you and the waiter, you should be able to communicate what you want fairly easily. You can also point to a meal that looks yummy at an adjacent table—though this is probably considered rude, so try to be discreet. It's true that you won't always receive what you *thought* you asked for, but "stay chill" as my daughter would say. At one restaurant on Sushi Street in Tokyo Station, I thought I was ordering six pieces of sushi—but actually ordered eighteen! I laughed and did my best to eat it all, reminding myself that it's not a moral imperative to send things back just because it wasn't what I expected.

Best Values

As you might guess, a restaurant's set meal can offer the best value for your money in Japan. Several times, Tessa and I ate what I consider fairly fancy multi-course dinners for under $50 for the two of us, and almost always the food was a much better value than what you'd find in the States.

A restaurant's set meals, or teishokus, are often excellent values, especially for lunch.

Lunch can be an especially screaming deal. Roy explains, "Somehow, lunch menus are very cheap in Japan, traditionally. One of the reasons might be that the business owners are using lunch menus as their advertisement. Some restaurants offer their lunch sets at the price of one-tenth of that of dinner menus. Don't be intimidated by the gorgeous facades of fancy restaurants. It doesn't hurt to just check the prices of their lunch set menus."

As proof of this, in Kanazawa, Tessa and I stumbled onto a small corner café near our hotel and ate a delicious, filling set lunch for about $7 each. We ran into a similar, delicious dumpling place in Sendai for about the same price.

友 ROY RECOMMENDS

Omakase, Izakaya, Kaiseki

"I assume many foreigners have watched YouTube or T.V. shows about omakase experiences. To be honest, the word is not common in our daily lives," Roy explains. "Of course, we Japanese know how the dishes are remarkably good if we splurge several thousand yen for one meal, but it's far from the down-to-earth cultural event.

"With less than one-tenth of the budget, I can easily take you to heaven with a visit to an izakaya. An izakaya is a Japanese version of a pub or Spanish tapas bar. People who have the most sensitive tongues are Japanese salarymen who have the opportunity to grab delicious meals that are paid for by their companies or, sometimes, clients. Izakaya culture has been nurtured by these people who call it 'meeting.' The red lantern is the sign of izakaya. If the izakaya is filled with men in black/navy suits, it is definitely the way to go

"Omakase means that the plates are all served by the chef's will," Roy continues. "Omakase can be a sushi course, a teppanyaki course, or a kaiseki course. Kaiseki especially looks extremely elegant and artistic. Every time a new plate is served, the guests sigh deeply. Kaisei is amazingly beautiful in appearance. It's so subtle. It's like a petal of cherry blossom on the river. But how does it taste? If 90% of your meals are Japanese and if your tongue knows the subtle differences of the cooking styles, ingredients, and methods, kaiseki is for you. On the other hand, if this is your first trip and you are not so familiar with Japanese cuisine, please don't expect too much from kaiseki. By request, I have brought many foreign guests to kaiseki restaurants, but have rarely heard positive feedback from them. I still recommend you make a kaiseki reservation as an experience, but probably once is enough."

Eat and Run

As mentioned, many Japanese restaurants serve only about fifteen people at a time and seem to have local, loyal clientele, so to avoid a line I recommend eating a bit earlier or later. This also raises an important point of etiquette: **at lunch places, eat your food and bug out**. Because these tiny places can't serve many people, they depend on a high turnover to make a profit. You don't need to be frantic about eating, but don't camp out in a place reading *The Japan Times*, either. Finish your meal and make room for the next customer.

How often you want to eat in a restaurant is totally up to you, and probably depends on your budget, how big of a foodie you are, and how much time you want to sit in one place. My daughter and I realized that our tolerance for "restaurant sitting" averaged about once per day, and we usually chose lunch to be our day's restaurant meal. This was partly because lunch is such a good value in Japan, but it's also because we were walking six to ten miles per day. By evening, we simply felt too tired to drag ourselves out to a place where we might have to stand in line and wait a while for our food.

Fortunately, Japan has some great alternatives to restaurants for the tired and hungry traveler.

NOODLE JOINTS

As popular as sit-down restaurants and cafés are in Japan, they are probably outnumbered by fast-serve ramen, udon, and other noodle places. For our very first meal in Japan, we walked from our hotel to Tokyo Station where we quickly ran into a little noodle nook. Jet-lagged and ravenous, we pounced on it.

As at many similar places in Japan, we ordered by selecting and paying for our meal with cash at an automated machine. After ordering, the machine spit out a ticket and we sat down to wait until the cook motioned to come get our bowls of noodles. To be honest, this first meal wasn't the greatest, but we paid less than $8 for both bowls, and it got some calories into our stomachs fast.

Fortunately, we had other, really delicious noodle meals later in the trip. I generally ordered my noodles with vegetables and a variety of pork, ham, and/or egg. My vegetarian daughter opted for tofu or just vegetables.

For the tired traveler, Japan's numerous noodle places offer a quick way to get a delicious, inexpensive meal.

Japan has several popular noodle chains and in Kyoto, we tried one of them, Ichiran Ramen. No queue was visible from the street and we thought we'd timed the crowds just right. Little did we know that a long line snaked down a hallway once we got inside the building! Those sneaky ramen guys!

We once again placed and paid for our orders on a machine, and then waited about twenty minutes until we got seated. The eating area was divided into little rooms full of semi-private booths where a person could eat his or her ramen in peace and anonymity. Arrays of lights in the hallway turned green when a booth became available, and when it was our turn, an attendant herded us to our gastronomic "confessionals."

When an anonymous chef slid my bowl into my booth, it was hot and delicious and I eagerly slurped it down. It wasn't even the best noodle bowl meal I had on the trip, but Tessa and I both savored it, and I recommend giving the Ichiran chain a try—especially since they have almost one hundred locations around the country. If you live in New York, you can get a head start and try one there!

友 *ROY RECOMMENDS*

Fast Food

While many foreign visitors might view it as a point of honor to avoid all American and other foreign restaurant chains, Roy insists that this is a mistake.

"Please try McDonald's once in Japan," he urges. "*What?* Yes, you should try McDonald's, Denny's, Starbucks, and Subway in Japan. They are the best places to compare Japan and the rest of the world. Especially I recommend you drop into Denny's. Japan Denny's has been a trend setter for the entire food industry of this country for many years. It was Denny's who brought juicy papaya, tiramisu, Nata de coco, pancake, etc . . . onto our table.

"Starbucks serves unique seasonally flavored drinks: cherry blossom in spring, chestnut in fall and, of course, special sweets for Halloween and Christmas. Don't miss MOS burger, Japan's original fast food chain. It's a counterpart of McDonald's. Their rice burgers were absolutely a game changer when they were released in 1987. Rice is used for hamburgers instead of buns. MOS Rice burgers are still sold to this day."

While I have to admit that Tessa and I failed to try McDonald's and Denny's while visiting, we became big fans of MOS Burger while visiting Taiwan in 2014. On our Japan trip, Tessa opted out because she is a vegetarian, but I took advantage of this uniquely Japanese fast food experience.

STREET FOOD

One of my big regrets is that I didn't try more street food in Japan. This was partly because, as noted before, my daughter is vegetarian and much of the street food contains meat. I did try several items including grilled scallops on a stick, some weird fried cheesy things, a bean-paste bun shaped like a fish (taiyaki), a hot apple custard pastry, and most memorably, green matcha ice-cream with extra matcha powder that, I suspect, was made by one of the big pharma companies responsible for the opioid epidemic. Most of these items were excellent.

Street food is safe to eat and easy to find in Japan, either from carts or established stalls and stores. Just a few of the places we encountered wonderful concentrations of street food included Tokyo's Tsukiji Outer Market, Kyoto's Nishiki Market, the main drag in Kamakura, and the street below the Zenkō-ji Temple in Nagano. Almost any place where large numbers of people gather, however, will have

Japan's 'street food' offers a great way to sample each area's specialties, such as these scrumptious custard apple pies in Nagano.

good street food, so take advantage of it. Tsukiji Market is especially known as a place to grab good sushi for breakfast, but can get very crowded so arrive early.

COFFEE SHOPS

Just as in the States or Europe, coffee shops are big business in Japan, and just like here, are good places to find quick meals such as croissants, sandwiches, yoghurt, and the like. Some have a better selection than others, but we found many to be remarkably uncrowded, making them a nice choice to chill out and recharge for a while. Plenty of good independent places are available, of course, but you'll find an abundance of Starbucks and other popular chains that include Doutor, Moriva, and Tully's. We especially liked the food selection at the Excelsior Caffe chain. Roy's favorite Japanese coffee shop chain is Ueshima Coffee. "It's like the Japanese counterpart of Starbucks. Ueshima Coffee's breakfast is always my first pick," he says.

CONVENIENCE STORES

You may be tempted to just skip this particular chapter—**but don't!** If you're like us and, I suspect, most other travelers, convenience stores will play a significant role in your Japan experience—and not

Japan's 50,000+ convenience stores are not only a staple of Japanese life, they are great places to grab some quick, good food. –Photo courtesy Roy Ozaki

just for their ATMs, toiletries, copier machines, postal services, and other basic supplies and services. They are also great places to go for good, cheap food!

As mentioned, Tessa and I were often too tired by the end of a day to drag ourselves out to a restaurant. More often than not, our solution was to stop by a convenience store and pick up a meal to eat back in our room.

Japan boasts more than *fifty thousand* convenience stores, and in urban and suburban areas, they seem to be located every couple of blocks–if not more frequently. There are three major chains: Family Mart, 7-Eleven, and Lawson's. Most operate 24 hours a day. They all offer the expected selection of chips, cookies, yoghurt, coffee, and soft drinks, but they also carry a surprising assortment of both cold and hot food. This includes sandwiches, fried chicken, dumplings, and much, much more.

I especially loved the rice balls, including those stuffed with either tuna or salmon and mayonnaise or cream cheese. Yum! I grabbed egg and tuna salad sandwiches on multiple occasions. Don't laugh, but it also took us going to Japan to discover Cup Noodles, despite how popular they've become in the States.

Convenience stores offer plenty of desserts to satisfy your sweet tooths including both packaged cookies and baked goods such as chocolate eclairs. One brand of cookie we fell in love with–or should I say, became addicted to–were the "Choco Ma-mi-re" cookies (ma-mi-re.jp) made by Fujiya foods. I have no doubt that we consumed enough of these to boost their stock price by several thousand yen. When I tired of cookies, I enjoyed exploring Meiji, Lotte, Morinaga, and Japan's other chocolate brands.

If you have a microwave at your hotel, be sure to try some of the frozen items found at convenience stores. I was especially impressed with some of the frozen dumplings I bought. Some convenience stores also have "sit down" areas where you can eat your purchases on the spot.

As noted before, you can use Suica, Pasmo, and other IC cards to purchase food at convenience stores, but they also accept credit cards and cash.

Almost daily, Tessa and I relied on convenience stores for quick meals and treats.

DEPA-CHIKA: FANCY FOOD FLOORS

While we're on the subject of desserts, one thing Tessa and I encountered several times were whole floors full of booths selling very fancy foods. They included fancy chocolates, other candies, pastries, and perhaps Japan's most famous fancy food, Tokyo Banana (think a Japanese take on a Twinkie). One of these markets occupied the entire ground floor of a department store at Tokyo Station, while another sprawled across the ground floor of a high-rise mall next to Shibuya Station. Being the chocoholics that we are, we intended to buy something at one of them—until we noticed that nine small truffles cost something in the neighborhood of forty or fifty bucks! Indeed, the items sold in these places seemed to emphasize elegance and packaging over anything else, and it became evident that many people were buying things as gifts. "They are called *depa-chika*," Roy explains, "which comes from 'Department store's underground (chika).' We go shopping in depa-chika for special occasions, like for souvenirs, gifts, tokens, and/or offerings for Buddhist altars. Of course, some rich people visit these shops as if they were visiting convenience stores, but basically a depa-chika is very special place for Japanese." I wasn't brave enough to buy something, but don't let that stop you. You may be in for a wonderful confectionary surprise.

VENDING MACHINES

If you are desperate for a quick pick-me-up, and in the almost inconceivable case that you can't find a convenience store nearby, one of the fun cultural features of Japan is the ascendancy of vending machines. In large cities, you will be hard-pressed to travel more than a couple hundred meters without passing one or more of these machines. Surprisingly, most of them don't sell food—but some of them do, especially candy, chips, and ice-cream. Their real strength is their huge variety of both hot and cold drinks, distinguished by red and blue labels above their buttons.

Some of the machines feature traditional soft drinks, but they also sell a delightful assortment of juices, energy drinks, coffees, and teas. Tessa forged a permanent relationship with hot milk tea, which provided her with both comfort and caffeine when she needed it throughout the day. Different companies operate different vending

In almost any urban area, thousands of vending machines are definitely "the boss" for grabbing milk tea and other drinks.

machines and one of the fun things Tessa did was try all of the different brands to find which ones she liked best.

Besides the drink vending machines, different machines can offer alcoholic beverages, hot ramen, and frozen food. You'll also find machines that sell underwear, adult magazines, toys, mystery prizes, Pokémon cards, and many other things—but don't eat those.

HOTEL BREAKFASTS

Choosing hotels with complimentary breakfasts can save you money, just as it can elsewhere. In general, we found Japan's free hotel breakfasts to be so-so, but they were certainly sufficient to fill us up before an arduous day of walking or travel.

Many hotels also offer breakfast for an additional fee, and unlike the free breakfasts, a couple of these turned out to be quite good. Our first hotel in Tokyo offered an expansive buffet featuring eggs, breakfast meats, fresh fruits, yoghurt, baked goods, green vegetables, and my favorite—fresh sushi.

Which brings up a point about breakfast in Japan. The country is not wedded to the traditional breakfast concepts we cling to in the

West. Besides the sushi, I especially loved that I could get a dose of steamed greens to start my day. Part of the Japan experience is to embrace the challenge of trying something different, and this presented a great opportunity.

The fancier breakfast I just mentioned cost us about $20, but we both considered it well worth it to help launch us out into the world. Other hotels charged about half that, so definitely give it some consideration.

JAPAN FOR VEGETARIANS

Vegetarians may wonder if they can find enough to eat in Japan. The country's cuisine, after all, heavily emphasizes beef, pork, chicken, and seafood. Fortunately, there are a lot of great options that don't have meat—especially different rice and noodle dishes. Ramen with

While I satisfied my cravings for tempura shrimp, my vegetarian teen hit only one or two bumps sticking to her vegetarian diet.

vegetables and/or egg is an easy thing to find, as is vegetable tempura. Hard-boiled or "tempura'ed" eggs are often served with meals, and dairy products are widespread.

Tofu is an especially common ingredient in many dishes including the ubiquitous miso soup. Be warned that tofu is sometimes served cold, to be eaten with soy sauce. Variations of sushi with fried tofu also are available. For more tofu information, check out the "Japanese Tofu" page at:

➤ **www.japan-guide.com**

All in all, my vegetarian teen didn't have any trouble finding enough to eat in Japan–though she did "fall off the wagon" once or twice so that she could sample some of Japan's more famous meat dishes. She quickly climbed back on board, however, and says she would return to Japan as a vegetarian in a plaque-free heartbeat!

ROY'S FINAL FOOD THOUGHTS

To round out our food discussion, I turn to Roy to provide the Big Picture of food throughout the country:

"Just as New York and Los Angeles are totally different from each other in so many ways, Tokyo and Kyoto/Osaka don't share a lot of common ground, including food culture. To be honest, the four-hundred year history of Tokyo is shallow and primitive in comparison with that of Kyoto/Osaka. Every time I dine out in Kyoto/Osaka, I discover that my tongue is childish. There are 47 prefectures in Japan, and the food in one prefecture is not the food you have eaten in the other prefecture, so I guarantee you won't ever get bored by Japanese cuisine, wherever you go."

Don't be surprised if you fall in love with Japan's famous electronic toilets, which are both hygienic to use and good for the environment.

PART VII

Health and Hygiene

楽

Japan Vaccine Requirements

In the wake of the pandemic, it bears repeating that it's a must to stay up on your vaccinations, and at least at the time of this writing, Japan wants to make sure people coming into the country have taken the proper precautions. Besides making sure you have your full complement of COVID-19 vaccinations, the CDC recommends you are up-to-date on what they call routine vaccinations such as chickenpox, DTP, flu, MMR, polio, and shingles. They also recommend getting vaccinated against hepatitis A & B and possibly other diseases depending on what you will be doing and where. **This is not a complete list, and you should look at the CDC website for Japan to make sure what you need.** Currently, this can be found at:

➤ **wwwnc.cdc.gov/travel/destinations/traveler/none/japan**

It's also important to know that the CDC list *is not* the Japan list, though the two have a lot of overlap. To understand what Japan requires for you to enter, check

Japan Travel:

➤ **www.japan.travel/en/guide/vaccines-for-japan/**

Japan Travel (covid):

➤ **www.japan.travel/en/practical-coronavirus-information/travelers/**

You should also look at the website for Japan's U.S. Embassy:

➤ **jp.usembassy.gov/services/welcomebacktojapan/**

As an extra precaution, check the latest coronavirus procedures detailed at the Ministry of Foreign Affairs of Japan page:

➤ **www.mofa.go.jp/ca/fna/page4e_001053.html**

If any of the above website addresses are broken by the time you try them, simply do web searches for subjects such as "required vaccinations for Japan" and "U.S. embassy Japan" and you will quickly find the updated websites. Do make sure you are looking at **official pages**, however, as blogs and commercial websites can quickly become out of date, even if they have the best intentions.

Although Japan may or may not require it, you will also want to carry copies of your complete vaccination records with you. This will not only help ensure that you are allowed into the country, it will come in handy if you come down with any unusual illnesses. Tessa and I took photos of our covid vaccination cards on our phones in case we lost the originals.

Check Your Medicines

To ensure your good health while in Japan, bring adequate supplies of all of your usual medicines. **However, do not assume that because your medicines are legal in the U.S. or elsewhere that they are legal in Japan.** Certain substances found in some cold medicines and anti-depressants, for instance, are illegal in Japan. Others may be legal to bring in, but cannot be obtained within the country. As a precaution, I did not bring any cold medicines into the country with me, but bought some tablets at a pharmacy when we arrived in case we needed them.

Up-to-date information on what is and isn't allowed can be found on the U.S. Embassy website listed on the previous page. There, you will also find a link for the appropriate page of the **Ministry of Health, Labour, and Welfare of Japan** (MHLW). You should read both of these sites carefully.

—image courtesy of the U.S. Embassy in Japan

If You Get Sick

In Part I, I discussed the advisability of buying travel insurance before you go to Japan—or any other country, for that matter. But what if you get sick while you're there? What do you do? Obviously, it depends on what's going on.

If you or someone else is in an accident, you can dial "119" on your phone, which should be easy to remember because it's the exact reverse of "911." Ambulances are free in Japan, and if one is required it will come and take you or a loved one to an emergency care facility. If the person answering your 119 call doesn't speak a lot of English, just remember the phrase "medical emergency" and they should be able to figure things out.

Once you are at a facility, the care you receive and how you pay for it will depend on your insurance. If at all possible, you should call your insurance company immediately to tell them the situation and ask what you should do next. **Make sure that you have your insurance card with you at all times so that if you are unconscious, the hospital can look through your belongings and know to call your insurance company.**

If it is not a critical emergency, but you feel ill and need a doctor, you will want to call your insurance for "pre-approval" of a doctor or facility to go to. With luck, you will not have to pay anything up front, but for some insurance you will probably need to pay and get reimbursed by your insurance company later. The **Japan Tourism Agency** has a useful "Guidebook for when you are feeling ill" that can be found at:

➤ **www.jnto.go.jp/emergency/common/pdf/guide_eng.pdf**

A safety information card can be found at:

➤ **www.mlit.go.jp/kankocho/content/001471575.pdf**

It's a good idea to print these out and take them with you.

An article with additional detailed information, including buying insurance once you've arrived in Japan, can be found on the **Live Japan** website at:

➤ **livejapan.com/en/article-a0002612/**

Hotel desks can also help you find a doctor or arrange for one to visit you.

The Miracle of Japanese Toilets

After food the, ahem, Number Two reason most people travel to Japan is to experience the miracle of Japanese toilets. Okay, maybe not. But these electronic *derrière* devices really are a joy to use. At their most basic, a Japanese toilet functions as a bidet—shooting water up into your nether regions to wash you clean after you've done your business. Especially for someone with hemorrhoids, this is wonderful because rubbing these regions with toilet paper often causes bleeding.

Japanese toilets, however, can do much more than just wash you clean. Depending on the model, they can also:

- Air-dry you after you've been washed.
- Heat up the toilet seat for you.
- Play background music or nature sounds while you are performing or pondering your next, ahem, move.
- Provide a "night light" to help you find your way in the dark.
- Automatically lift and lower the seat.
- Automatically clean and deodorize themselves.
- And more.

Some of these features are based on proximity and motion detectors that sense when you enter the bathroom or sit down or stand up. The first time I walked into a bathroom at night and the lid automatically lifted, I almost ran away in fright—but you'll be amazed how quickly you get used to it. It does make you ask why the rest of the world hasn't lovingly embraced these devices. Not only are Japanese toilets more hygienic than using toilet paper, they are much more environmentally friendly. Even though the toilets use a bit of extra water to wash you off, much more water—not to mention wood and energy—is used to process trees into toilet paper.

In our travels, we found that many of the electronic controls for Japanese toilets had only the Japanese language written on them, but helpful little diagrams made clear what most of the buttons did. At hotels, additional instructions in English are often posted on the wall next to the toilet—leaving you to fully enjoy one of Japan's more wonderful, wetter pleasures.

Doing Laundry

Whenever I am packing for a trip of more than a day or two, one of my considerations is how many clothes to bring. That, in turn, makes me wonder how easy it will be to do laundry where I am going. If that is also spinning through your mind, I've got good news for you: **Doing laundry in Japan is easy!**

Every hotel we stayed at had clean, functional self-serve washers and dryers at very reasonable prices, eliminating even the temptation to hand wash socks and underwear in the bathroom sink. Just as good, some hotels will do your laundry for you at much more reasonable prices than what you'd find at a hotel in the West. At a typical hotel in the States, getting a single tee-shirt washed might cost you the price of a cheap lunch. In one Japan hotel we stayed at, they washed, dried, and folded our entire load of laundry for less than ten bucks. Now that's how travelers should be treated!

That said, we usually decided to do our laundry ourselves and it never cost more than three or four bucks a load. Here are a few notes that might help:

- Make sure you have—or obtain—some 100-yen coins and sometimes even smaller change to put in the machines.
- Many hotels provide soap free of charge for you to use in the machines.
- If you can't figure out where to add the soap in a washing machine, there's a good chance that it automatically dispenses the soap itself. Uh, *why* don't we have machines like that in America?
- Hotel machines tend to be a bit smaller capacity than your home washer and dryer, so be prepared to do more than one load if you have a backlog of laundry.
- As always, leave a laundry room as clean or cleaner than you found it, and with the door securely closed so that the noise of the machines won't bother other hotel guests.

And that nicely leads us into our next step . . .

One great thing about Japan is that if you need something, shopping is always just a few steps away.

Less is more while traveling Japan, and the country is ideally suited for travel with small roller suitcases. (Kanazawa Station shown here.)

PART VIII

Packing

楽

Clothing and Other Items to Bring

Okay, you know what I'm going to say here, right? *What you pack for Japan depends on what you'll be doing there, what time of year you'll be going, and how long you plan to stay.* If you have traveled anywhere at all in your lifetime, you already know this. Planning for Japan, though, merits some particular packing considerations. Let's begin with the basics.

My general rule of thumb is to take enough clothes so that I can survive for a week without doing laundry. That doesn't necessarily mean that I bring seven sets of everything. In a temperate climate such as Japan in spring or fall, I usually find I can get away with occasionally wearing shirts and underwear more than once, and pants three or four times, if not more. For our three-week trip at the end of March and beginning of April, here are the basic clothing items I took, *including* what I wore on the plane:

- ☐ 1 hat
- ☐ 3 quick-dry (synthetic) tee-shirts
- ☐ 2 polo-type shirts
- ☐ 1 (rugged) long-sleeve shirt
- ☐ 5 sets of underwear
- ☐ 7 pairs of socks
- ☐ 1 nice-looking pullover/sweatshirt
- ☐ 1 light raincoat
- ☐ 2 pairs of long cargo pants
- ☐ 1 pair sweatpants
- ☐ 1 pair of shorts
- ☐ 1 pair of shoes
- ☐ 1 pair of flip-flops
- ☐ 1 swimsuit

Believe it or not, this ended up being a bit of overkill. The ease of doing laundry in Japan (see last chapter) means that I could have left behind at least a couple pairs of socks and underwear, one or two shirts, and probably my spare pair of cargo pants. Still, all of the above fit comfortably into my carry-on suitcase (see next chapter).

Of course, this is a clothing list geared toward a casual traveler. If you plan to go out to fancy restaurants or visit the emperor, well, you're on your own. Still, the above type of list should work well for the vast majority of travelers, with probably a few modifications if you happen to be a different gender. My daughter, for instance, packed in terms of "outfits"—three or four of them—instead of individual shirts and pants. She also opted for two pairs of shoes.

Speaking of shoes, let's talk about them before we discuss other items you'll want to bring. **When traveling, shoes are the key to all happiness**, and before our trip, I realized that I did not have an adequate pair for our journey. I needed something sturdy and comfortable enough for me to walk a lot, but also something that looked nice enough to wear (or take off) in restaurants, museums, temples, and so forth. Furthermore, I was determined to bring only *one* pair of shoes, so it had to meet all of the aforementioned requirements.

On trips where I'm going to do a lot of hiking on trails or rough terrain, I almost always opt for a pair of light hiking boots. On big city pavement, however, even light boots grow heavy, hot, and painful in a hurry so I wanted something cooler and more comfy. After buying and trying two much more expensive pairs of footwear, I found a discontinued $50 pair of Skechers that exactly fit my needs. They were sturdy and lightweight. They had lots of internal padding. As a bonus, they were black, so that they would look decent in almost any situation.

Believe me, I put these shoes through the paces. During our three-week visit, we walked about 150 miles, including a couple of hikes on slightly rough terrain. I'm happy to report that the shoes performed like Patrick Mahomes in the Super Bowl—without the ankle injury. Which shoes work for you will depend on your feet and preferences. The main point here: *Make sure your shoes will feel comfortable pounding the pavement day after day, and test them thoroughly before you go.*

With that essential out of the way, what else should you bring? Well, obviously, your important documents, medicines, phone, money, credit cards, and itinerary that we've discussed in previous chapters. Besides those, here is the rest of my suggested list:

- ☐ Sunglasses
- ☐ Headlamp flashlight
- ☐ Toilet kit (toothbrush, razor, clippers, etc . . .)
- ☐ 2 or 3 larger mesh and/or plastic bags for dirty laundry, and sundries
- ☐ Basic first-aid kit with adhesive bandages, antacids, ibuprofen, etc . . .
- ☐ Journal/diary
- ☐ Japan guidebook(s)—including this one, of course!
- ☐ Book to read
- ☐ Refillable water bottle
- ☐ Money belt (optional, see "Money" in Part IV)
- ☐ Fanny pack
- ☐ Handkerchiefs
- ☐ Personal electronic devices
- ☐ Chargers for your devices (see electricity chapter)
- ☐ Small empty duffel bag to carry souvenirs home (see next chapter)
- ☐ Small portable umbrella (see below)

You'll note that the list contains no liquids of any kind and, regarding that, you'll have to decide ahead of time whether you plan to check your baggage or carry it on the plane with you. If you check it, you probably can pack shampoo, sunscreen, gels, makeup, and other non-hazardous liquids in your suitcase. If you opt for carry-on you will, at the time of this writing, only be able to bring very small bottles (3.4 ounces/100 ml or less each). These must be placed together in a quart-sized zipped plastic bag that you can easily pull out for inspection when you go through security. For the latest regulations, be sure to check the TSA website:

➤ **www.tsa.gov/travel/security-screening/liquids-rule**

Keep in mind that every place you stay at in Japan will have shampoo, conditioner, and lotion. Rather than messing with these and other liquids, I recommend just hitting a Family Mart or other convenience store when you arrive and picking up toothpaste, sunscreen, deodorant, and other sundries.

Speaking of convenience stores, as soon as we arrived we also bought collapsible **umbrellas**—something I highly recommend. Raincoats are required, but if the rain is really crashing down, as it often does in Asia, you are going to want the added protection of an umbrella, too. It ended up raining on only two days of our trip, but during those two days we thanked the convenience store gods for our umbrellas over and over again.

Besides everything we've discussed in this chapter, whatever else you bring is totally up to you. Just remember that you will be traveling in a very modern, civilized country and if you forget anything or feel you need anything, you will most likely be able to obtain it almost anywhere you go. **In short, get your essentials packed—and then don't worry about it**.

Also keep in mind that you will want to leave room in your luggage for bringing home gifts and souvenirs for yourself and others. In fact, I packed one fewer tee-shirts than I thought I might need because I fully expected to buy and wear a Japan tee on the trip. That, of course, leads in nicely to the question of luggage and just how much space you'll have to work with.

Luggage

On most adventurous trips where I'll be roughing it or having to carry my stuff long distances, I have opted for a regular internal-frame (soft) backpack, and during our trip we certainly saw other travelers with large backpacks. For the vast majority of travelers to Japan, however, an **overhead-sized roller suitcase** is the way to go. Why? Because, at least for your first trip, you will find that almost everywhere you visit will have smooth surfaces ideal for pulling along a roller suitcase. Not only that, on your many train rides, you will want to be able to easily stash your suitcase in an overhead rack. Conversely, if you are on a subway or bus, you will want a bag that is compact enough to keep out of the way of other people.

For our trip, we decided to splurge on new suitcases. I purchased a Samsonite Freeform 21-inch hardside suitcase with double spinner wheels, and bought Tessa an Amazon Basics 21-inch Hardside Spinner. We were both extremely pleased with our choices. Both suitcases proved durable and handled well whether we pulled or pushed them. They also had the right amount of room for our stuff—with a bit left over for extra Japan purchases.

If you look at my list in the previous chapter, you'll notice that I also packed an **empty medium-sized mesh duffel**. This folded down into almost nothing, but came in incredibly useful as we headed down our final stretch toward home. That's because we could cram all of our gifts and souvenirs into it. Quite consciously, we waited until the last few days of our trip to make most of our purchases so that we wouldn't have to drag them all across Japan. Once we got to our final Tokyo hotel, though, we cut loose and basically filled up the extra duffel.

In addition to my suitcase, I also brought a **medium-sized daypack**. In this I carried our itinerary and reservations, my book and journal, camera, iPad, chargers, first-aid kit, water bottle, hat, sunglasses, maps, travel guide, snacks, and sweatshirt—when I wasn't wearing it. Mostly, I carried this daypack only when we were traveling from one hotel location to another, and then left it in our room. For our daily outings, I generally brought only water and maps with us, putting them into the **fanny pack** that I also brought along on the trip—something that I also highly recommend. On these outings, Tessa usually carried a nylon bag with a drawstring—something just large enough for her journal and the bottles of milk tea that she inevitably purchased from vending machines each day.

To recap, here is a list of luggage and what we used each for:

- 21-inch carry-on roller suitcase (clothes, toiletries)
- Daypack (books, electronics, itinerary, headlamp, water bottle, hat, sweatshirt)
- Fanny pack (water, maps, snacks during outings)
- Light, foldable duffel (souvenirs and other purchases to bring home)

Electricity and Electronics

As you are debating what to bring with you on your trip, you will naturally be wondering what kind of electricity Japan has and if you need to buy an adapter of some kind. The good news is that Japan's electricity system is perfectly suitable for most, if not all, U.S. appliances and devices. Japan's electricity runs at 100 volts—close enough to our own 120 that it is unlikely to damage any of your electric components. Just to be sure, check that your devices are rated down to 100 volts by looking at the fine print on the plug of your chargers. If a plug says it needs, say, 120 volts instead of being in the 100- to 120-volt range, you should probably bring a 100V to 120V adapter with you. Note that Tessa and I recharged our phones, tablet, headphones, and electric razors without any problems.

Of course, you need to be able to plug your devices into an outlet, too. Almost all of the electrical outlets you will encounter in Japan are Type A, the "two-prong" type, meaning that most of us can just plug in the vast majority of our chargers. **However, if you bring something that requires a "three-prong," or Type B, outlet, you should bring your own "two-prong to three-prong" adapter with you**.

One quirk of Japan's electricity grid is that in eastern Japan, electricity runs at 50 hertz (Hz) while in western Japan, it runs at 60 hertz, like it does in the States. If you are in eastern Japan, this difference will not damage your equipment, but it may mean that electric clocks may not keep the proper time.

One final question you might be asking is, "Should I bring a computer?" Unless you are traveling for work, I wouldn't. I brought our ancient iPad simply because it is easier to make or change reservations, respond to urgent emails, and things like that on a bigger device. An actual computer, though, is one more expensive thing that can be lost, damaged, or stolen—and if you can't find enough to do in Japan without having yours with you, well, you aren't trying very hard! One of the things I love about travel is having more time to read real books and write in my journal. That's much harder to do when your "mothership connection" is sitting right next to you.

Posing near one of our favorite Japan places, the Kamo River in Kyoto.

PART IX

Get Ready for Fun

楽

You're going to love Japan. Really. No matter why you originally chose to go there, if you keep an open mind, be your best self, and take time to pay attention to what's around you, you will have memories that will never leave you. You may end up loving the country for entirely different reasons than you expected, and if so, all the better. Whatever wonderful experiences you have, I hope this book has helped you prepare for your journey—and other journeys to come.

Although this is not a sightseeing book, I've tried to drop in little things that we especially enjoyed, but now it's time to do one better and give you our and Roy's actual "Favorite Things" lists. I can almost guarantee that what *we* loved most will be at least a little different than what *you* will love most—but I hope our lists will get your imagination churning. For more ideas, you will also want to check out the resources at the end of this book, many of which I have already mentioned.

If you are grappling a bit with how to allocate your time, I have also included our basic itinerary to give you some ideas. And in case you are wondering, the number of days we spent in each location turned out to be just about right, neither leaving us longing for more or feeling like we were way too rushed.

My final advice? Embrace it all and savor each moment, even when you encounter difficulties. Travel is fun—usually a *lot* of fun—but it is also a remarkable chance to learn about the world and yourself. From the moment you land, don't miss a moment.

SNEED'S AND TESSA'S TOP 25 EXPERIENCES IN JAPAN

(MOSTLY NON-FOOD AND IN NO PARTICULAR ORDER)

- Walking along the Kamo River in Kyoto
- Seeing blooming sakura trees almost everywhere
- Watching the Yokohama DeNA Baystars defeat the Yomiuri Giants in Tokyo Dome
- Visiting Kanazawa Castle Park and the adjacent Kenrokuen Garden
- Picking out food at convenience stores
- Riding the Enoshima Electric Railway

- Exploring the island of Enoshima
- Kiyomizu-dera Temple, Kyoto
- Visiting Character Street, Ramen Street, and the rest of Tokyo Station
- Spending a day exploring Sendai on foot
- Fushimi Inari Taisha Shrine, Kyoto
- Milk tea and vending machines
- Kamakura
- Visiting the Hachiko statue at Shibuya Crossing
- Train rides from Kyoto to Kanazawa, and Kanazawa to Nagano
- Shinjuku Gyoen National Garden, Tokyo
- Watching a sumo wrestling tournament on television
- Visiting Kyoto's Arashiyama Park and bamboo grove
- Strolling Ueno Park, Tokyo
- Shopping Shibuya's "skyscraper malls"
- Wandering Kanazawa's Higashi Chaya teahouse and geisha district
- Eating sushi for breakfast
- Exploring Tokyo's Tsukiji Outer Market
- Kyoto's International Manga Museum
- Walking Shibuya at night

SNEED'S AND TESSA'S BASIC ITINERARY

TOKYO (TOKYO STATION AREA): NIGHTS 1-5

KAMAKURA: NIGHTS 6-8

KYOTO: NIGHTS 9-12

KANAZAWA: NIGHTS 13-14

NAGANO: NIGHT 15

TOKYO (SHIBUYA): NIGHTS 16-19

ROY'S "INSIDER"
TOP THINGS TO DO IN JAPAN
(IN NO PARTICULAR ORDER)

- Minakami Sanso (onsen ryokan)[9]
- Takaragawa Onsen Osenkaku (ryokan)
- Tenka-chaya restaurant (Mt Fuji viewing)
- Sanroku-en Japanese restaurant (thatched house near Lake Kawaguchi)
- Itchiku Kubota Museum by Lake Kawaguchi
- Maple Corridor by Lake Kawaguchi (great for fall visitors)
- Tokyo Restaurant Bus (lunch/dinner)
- Oku Shiga ski resort
- Hannoki Forest Museum in Oshino Hakkai
- Osesaki diving spot in Shizuoka
- Izu Shirahama, Nanki Shirahama (white sand beaches)
- Enoshima Island Spa
- Daikoku parking area (car enthusiasts, think "Fast and Furious" JDM meeting)
- Tokyo Gate Bridge
- Mikazuki Japanese Resorts & Spa
- Mother Farm (farming themed amusement park, great for kids)
- Hirizo Beach (snorkeling) in Izu Peninsula
- State Guesthouse Kyoto with English guidance
- Chojiya tororo (yam) jiru restaurant in Shizuoka
- Chanoma Tea Terrace in Shizuoka
- Tamiya headquarters in Shizuoka (plastic model company)
- Ishikawa Brewery, Tokyo (sake and beer in a historical setting)
- Chusonji Temple in Hiraizumi
- Unmanned grocery stores in the middle of nowhere

---

[9] Ryokans are traditional Japanese inns that can offer guests a more authentic Japanese experience. They can vary from very simple to very fancy, and some have onsens attached to them.
To learn more, visit www.japan.travel/en/guide/japanese-ryokan/

Japan Book and Website Travel Resources

Despite the wealth of travel resources to be found on the internet, I still turn to a physical travel book as my first step in researching a place I'd like to visit. Different people prefer different "brands" of guides, but *Lonely Planet Japan* provides an excellent overview of the country, its history, and customs. Unfortunately, the sheer quantity of information in this and other mainstream Japan travel and sightseeing guides can be pretty overwhelming—and is largely why I wrote this book—so you may also want to check out a "thinner" guide. Many of these are self-published and not worth the investment, but I did enjoy Ken and Yuki Fukuyama's *Things I Wish I Knew Before Going to Japan* and *14 Days in Japan* published by IDtravelling. *The Tokyo Cheapo e-Book* (tokyocheapo.com/book/) is a downloadable guidebook that I haven't read, but I love their website so am assuming the guidebook also is awesome.

In much simpler times, it used to be that traditional travel guides also were the best places to get information on hotels, restaurants, and sights, and they still can be useful in this regard. These days, however, online sources offer a wealth of information that is often more up-to-date and more accurate than what physical guidebooks can keep up with. Because of this, I recommend a "dual strategy" of using physical guidebooks to learn about Japan's basic history, culture, regions, and things to see—and websites and blogs for researching hotels, restaurants, ticket information, transportation, and the latest entry and health requirements. Below are online sources, organized by topic, that I found especially helpful. The links below were accurate at the time of publication, but if any of them have changed or no longer work, a simple web search such as "Japan Web" or "Japan Rail Pass" will quickly get you there. **Note that I did not accept any fees or other compensation for including any of the resources below or anywhere else in this book.**

ALL-AROUND USEFUL WEBSITES

The **Japan National Tourism Organization** (Japan.travel), which I'll refer to as "**Japan.travel**" from now on, is a great first stop for researching your journey. Their website offers extensive information for

Tokyo's Akihabara area is particularly popular with young people, who flock to the area for its gaming parlors and manga cafes.

visitors, from visa and airport information to detailed web pages for all of Japan's major cities. **Japan-guide.com** is another excellent site loaded with visitor information about destinations and trip planning, including great information about transportation. **Tokyo Cheapo** (Tokyocheapo.com) is an especially fun resource for looking up hotels, restaurants, activities, transportation and most other things you can think of. This site excels at recommending things for budget travelers, but all potential visitors should take a look. **Live Japan** (livejapan.com) and **Japan Talk** (japan-talk.com) are two other solid all-around sources of information.

ENTRY REQUIREMENTS, HEALTH, AND SAFETY

It's especially essential to check visa, vaccination, and other requirements before traveling to other countries, and Japan is no exception. Japan's latest entry requirements can be found at the website of the **Japan Ministry of Foreign Affairs** (www.mofa.go.jp/j_info/visit/visa/). Visitors from the U.S. and select other countries also will want to enter your immigration and customs information on **Japan Web** (vjw-lp.digital.go.jp/en/) *before your trip*. If you don't do this ahead of time, you will have to do it upon arrival—not something you want to deal with when you are jetlagged and stressed about entering a new country.

For information on vaccines and other health information, look up Japan on the **Centers for Disease Control** website (wwwnc.cdc.gov/travel/destinations/traveler/none/Japan).

For the latest security and safety concerns, check the **U.S. Department of State** website (www.state.gov/countries-areas/japan/).

Information on these topics can also be found on the **Japan.travel** website.

TRAINS AND TRANSPORTATION

The **Japan Rail Pass** website (japanrailpass.net/en/) provides extensive, detailed information about various rail pass options and how to purchase them. **Japan-guide.com** has great pages explaining IC cards (japan-guide.com/e/e2359_003.html) as well as the huge variety of local and regional rail passes available throughout the country (japan-guide.com/e/e2357.html). **Tokyo Metro** (www.tokyometro.jp/en/index.html) provides information about the "Welcome Tokyo" subway passes, Pasmo cards, and other facets of using subways. **Tokyo Cheapo** has oodles of information on all kinds of transport in and around the capital including a great article about Suica cards at tokyocheapo.com/travel/suica-card-guide/.

One of my favorite resources is the YouTube site of **ONE GOOD DREAM** at:

➤ www.youtube.com/@ONEGOODDREAM

Yoko, the producer, has narrated terrific videos about how to navigate various transportation challenges including buying shinkansen tickets and the best ways to get from Haneda and Narita airports into Tokyo.

Information for airport limousines can be found at:

➤ **webservice.limousinebus.co.jp/web/en/Top.aspx**

Information and links for long-distance buses can be found at:

➤ **www.japan.travel/en/plan/getting-around/buses/**

HOTELS

Many hotel web searches will come up with lists of luxury hotels that are beyond the reach of ordinary travelers. However, as mentioned in Step 5 of "Part II: A Japan Game Plan," **Booking.com** is a tremendous resource for finding hotels, providing best available prices and accurate reviews–as long as they have improved their recent, questionable business practices (see page 33). **TripAdvisor** (TripAdvisor.com) also does an excellent job presenting and reviewing hotels by cost, quality, and other criteria. **Tokyo Cheapo** carries reviews for a lot of hotels, hostels, and other lodging that may not show up on larger sites. **Airbnb** (Airbnb.com) also has a decent presence in Japan, with listings for rooms, apartments, and houses operated by private individuals. Though I have never actually booked with them, **Hotels.com** (Hotels.com) and **Japanican** (japanican.com) offer the same kinds of user-friendly search features.

You can, of course, go directly to various hotel websites as well as those of hotel chains. American chains tend to be very expensive in Japan, but Japan has its own chains that cater to the whole gamut of travelers (see Roy's list in **"Part II, Step 5: Group Your Activities by Location and Book Accommodations"**). You can find links to these by looking up a particular hotel chain or "Hotel chains in Japan" on Wikipedia. When we visited Nagano, for instance, we stayed in the **Sotetsu Fresa Inn Nagano**, which was a short walk from the JR shinkansen station. The room was simple, but clean and comfortable, and came with breakfast–all for about $90. Learn more at Sotetsu-hotels.com. We also stayed at the **Shibuya Tobu Hotel**, part of the Tobu hotel chain (www.tobuhotel.co.jp/en/), and were completely satisfied. Note that **Japan Railways** owns and operates more than 80 of its own hotels throughout the country (japanrailpass.net/en/hotel.html).

In big cities, don't forget Japan's famous capsule hotels, in which you basically rent a little tube or cubby for a night. These are especially great for individual travelers and, I'm told, can be quite comfy. We made a reservation at the highly recommended **Nine Hours Suidobashi** capsule hotel in Tokyo, but decided not to fritter away our precious time changing hotels. You can get a complete list of capsule hotels with a quick web search.

Japan.travel lists additional hotel reservation sites at www.japan.travel/en/online-reservation-sites.

RESTAURANTS

TripAdvisor, **TokyoCheapo**, **Lonely Planet**, and scores–maybe thousands–of other websites will give you recommendations for where to eat in Japan. The topic is worthy of several books and beyond the scope of this one. Simply do a search "Eating in Japan" or "Best restaurants in (location)." It also is worth consulting your physical guidebooks and hotel desks for restaurant recommendations. If you're out wandering around and you see a long line, chances are that it's a restaurant worth checking out!

SELECTED SPECIAL EVENTS/ ATTRACTIONS MENTIONED IN THIS BOOK

Studio Ghibli tickets: ghibli-museum.jp/en/tickets/

Yomiuri Giants (**baseball**) tickets: giants.jp/en/schedule/

Tokyo Disney: tokyodisneyresort.jp/en/ticket/

Sumo schedule and ticket Information: sumo.or.jp//En/

Kyoto International Manga Museum: kyotomm.jp/en/

Sunrise Express sleeper train:
www.jrailpass.com/blog/night-trains-sunrise-express

TRAVEL INSURANCE

Although I've purchased travel insurance, I have fortunately never had to use it. As a result, I can't recommend which providers may be better than others. I bought our insurance through **Travel Guard** (travelguard.com), and it seemed pretty straightforward. They also answered the phone immediately when I called with questions about the policy–a good sign. That said, I recommend doing a search on "Best Travel Insurance Companies" and studying reviews before making a purchase.

SOCIAL MEDIA SITES

Besides the above resources, I'd be remiss not to mention that plenty of social media sites offer up-to-date travel information and allow you to ask questions to other travelers. Two that I especially like are "Japan Travel, Friendly Discussion Group" and "Japan Travel Advice" on Facebook. The latter also runs **Tokiotours** (tokiotours.com) in case you'd like to take a fun bicycle, food, or other tour in Tokyo, Kyoto, or another popular Japanese city.

THANK YOU!

As fun and fascinating as researching this book proved to be, I am extremely grateful for the expert input from Lisa Chu-Thielbar and, of course, Roy Ozaki, whose contributions truly make this guide a one-of-a-kind experience. I would also like to thank Jeannie Painter for creating this guide's elegant and appealing design, and to my wife, Amy, for supporting my traveling obsession and for meticulously proofing the final draft. A big shout out to Paulette Parpart of the Missoula Public Library for assembling the book's cataloging information. Most of all, I'd like to thank my teen, Tessa, for her enthusiasm and interest in visiting Japan, and for being the ideal travel companion for our (hopefully not) once-in-a-lifetime journey.

Tessa with our very helpful travel concierge, Maki Shoji, of the Sendai Tourist Information Center.

Sneed B. Collard III is the author of more than 90 award-winning books, from the children's picture books *Birds of Every Color* and *Border Crossings*, to his adult memoir *Warblers & Woodpeckers: A Father-Son Big Year of Birding*, and his beginning birding guide *Birding for Boomers—and Everyone Else Brave Enough to Embrace the World's Most Rewarding and Frustrating Activity.* In addition to being a veteran traveler, Sneed has written more than one hundred articles about travel, nature, and the environment, and is a regular contributor to *Bird Watcher's Digest*, *Montana Outdoors*, *Big Sky Journal*, and the online magazine *Perceptive Travel.* Learn more about Sneed at his website www.sneedbcollardiii.com and by reading the blog he writes with his son, FatherSonBirding.com.

Ryosuke (Roy) Ozaki studied sociology and anthropology at Shizuoka University, and has lived in Japan for more than fifty years. As a chauffeur and tour guide, he enjoyed giving foreign visitors an inside perspective on his country and learned the kinds of things that most appeal to Japan's first-time visitors. Roy owns and operates the Mermaid Terrace (facebook.com/MermaidTerrace) in Hayama, a gathering place where both locals and travelers can spend quality time in a relaxing, refreshing atmosphere—with a view of Mount Fuji across the water. He also teaches English and swimming part-time, and continues to offer individual guiding services in Japan as time permits. To get in touch, contact him at deathorlaura@icloud.com.

NOTES

NOTES